W9-AXO-458

The
I DON'T UNDERSTAND
FOOTBALL

BOOK

Or

How to Tackle the Game Painlessly

Marvin Norinsky and
Margaret Gudmundsson

Illustrated by Ron and
Ronda Hildebrand

BEAUFORT BOOKS, INC.
New York   /   Toronto

Copyright © 1981 by Marvin Norinsky and Margaret Gudmundsson
All rights reserved. No part of this publication may be reproduced or transmitted in
any form or by any means, electronic or mechanical, including photocopy,
recording, or any information storage or retrieval system now known or to be
invented, without permission in writing from the publisher, except by a reviewer
who wishes to quote brief passages in connection with a review written for inclusion
in a magazine, newspaper, or broadcast.

Library of Congress Cataloging in Publication Data

Norinsky, Marvin.
   The I don't understand football book, or, How to tackle the game painlessly.
   1. Football—Anecdotes, facetiae, satire, etc.
I. Gudmundsson, Margaret. II. Title.
GV950.5. N67   796.332'0207   81-2744
ISBN 0-8253-0069-X AACR2

Published in the United States by Beaufort Books, Inc., New York.
Published simultaneously in Canada by General Publishing Co. Limited

Design by Ellen Lo Giudice
Printed in the United States of America   First Edition
10 9 8 7 6 5 4 3 2

Contents

Introduction

Every year, sometime around the middle of the summer, a strange malady afflicts a large portion of the population of North America. This disorder is characterized by trancelike states, glassy eyes, the consumption of large volumes of beer, a loss of interest in sexual activities, and an apparent lapse of short-term memory for promises and schedules. This is football madness, or in medical terms, *Porcus Epidermamania*.

The affliction appears to affect mainly, but not exclusively, members of the male gender. Although many women are affected, they constitute a relatively small proportion of the possessed. By far the largest majority are males between the ages of seven and eighty-seven.

The real victims, however, are the silent majority, the family members who don't share in the obsession. They see the effects all around them in the form of unmown lawns, unpainted fences, unchopped wood, unfulfilled sexual desires.

This book is written for all the suffering wives, lovers, husbands, neglected children, and thousands of lawns, fences, and what have you, in the hope that the pain and suffering can be alleviated, not by curing the malady, which like the common cold has no known cure, but by an injection of the virus itself. We base this therapy on the time-honored concept, "if you can't lick 'em, join 'em."

1

What It Was Was Football

From the backwoods of North Carolina came a twinkle-eyed country teacher, who, armed with an open, ingenuous face and a first-rate mountain twang, recorded the story of a naive hill dweller. In a visit to the big city he is caught up in the tidal movement of a crowd and finds himself in the stands of a packed and screaming stadium. There he witnesses two groups of oversized men grappling with intent to maim for possession of a strangely shaped orange object. And no sooner does one side have it than the other side tries to take it away again. *What It Was Was Football* started the career of Andy Griffith, who went on to stardom in films and on television.

To the uninitiated, Griffith's observations make perfect sense. Football does indeed look like an unorchestrated free-for-all between gigantic Neanderthals, encased in body armor, emblazoned with heraldic devices and magical numbers, grunting and groaning like sumo wrestlers as they attempt to crush each other's bodies before tens of thousands of spectators.

To the aficionado, however, what occurs on the one-hundred-yard greensward is a classical combination of chess, ballet, and war. The clash of the giants on the gridiron takes on the heroics of the clashes before the walls of Troy. The sports columnists and television color men take on the collective mantle of Homer, complete with that fabled poet's blindness.

So, you ask, where lies the truth? And that, my child, leads to the imponderable. The truth is in the eye of the beholder. To know the truth, it is necessary first to understand what you are seeing; then, judge for yourself.

THE TEAMS

The modern version of the professional game began in, of all places, Canton, Ohio, in the year 1920. Until then, although there had been "professional" teams since 1894, the game was still a "game" played on the fields of Harvard, Yale, Princeton, and even Lawrenceville, New Jersey, if we are to believe Booth Tarkington. In 1920, just two years after the Great War to End All Wars ended in Europe, the seeds of the Great Wars of Autumn were planted in a small industrial city in Ohio. Like so many innovators, the founding fathers of the American Professional Football Association could not have foreseen the impact of their actions.

A list of the first franchised teams tells an interesting story, as does the cost of these charter franchises, one hundred dollars. The teams were:

The Canton Bulldogs	Canton, Ohio
The Dayton Triangles	Dayton, Ohio
The Akron Professionals	Akron, Ohio
The Massillon Tigers*	Massillon, Ohio
The Rochester Jeffersons	Rochester, N.Y.

The Muncie?*	Muncie, Ind.
The Rock Island Independents	Rock Island, Ill.
The Decatur Staleys	Decatur, Ill.
The Buffalo All Americans	Buffalo, N.Y.
The Columbus Panhandles	Columbus, Ohio
The Detroit Heralds	Detroit, Mich.
The Chicago Tigers	Chicago, Ill.
The Cleveland Panthers	Cleveland, Ohio
The Chicago Cardinals	Chicago, Ill.
The Hammond Pros	Hammond, Ind.

*Massillon and Muncie were never able to field a team.

Of this charter group of teams, only two still exist. In 1922, George Halas moved the Decatur Staleys to Chicago and renamed them the Chicago Bears. Papa Bear Halas coached, played end, and owned the team as well. He still owns it. The Chicago Cardinals exist today as the St. Louis Cardinals. That same year (1922), with the demise of some teams and the addition of new ones, notably the Green Bay Packers, the association changed its name to the National Football League.

In 1970, the upstart American Football League merged with the senior league and formed the expanded National Football League made up of two major conferences, the National Football Conference and the American Football Conference. Both conferences were then broken up into three divisions. These divisions were theoretically regional by design. However, it appears that some people in high places in the league failed geography in grade school. Exactly what Dallas, deep in the heart of Texas, is doing in the Eastern Division of the NFC is a much a mystery as what Atlanta is doing in the Western Division of the same NFC. The AFC does a little better. They "snuck" Kansas City, located near the geographic center of the country, into the Western Division. That appears to be the only anomaly, but we advise that you keep your eyes open. If you live on the East Coast and find your city drifting west, telephone the NFL and demand they cease and desist.

The league breaks up thusly:

American Conference West	*National Conference West*
San Diego Chargers	San Francisco '49ers
Denver Broncos	Atlanta Falcons
Oakland Raiders	Los Angeles Rams
Kansas City Chiefs	New Orleans Saints
Seattle Sea Hawks	

American Conference Central	*National Conference Central*
Pittsburgh Steelers	Detroit Lions
Houston Oilers	Tampa Bay Buccaneers
Cincinnati Bengals	Chicago Bears
Cleveland Browns	Green Bay Packers
	Minnesota Vikings

American Conference East	*National Conference East*
Buffalo Bills	Philadelphia Eagles
Baltimore Colts	Dallas Cowboys
Miami Dolphins	New York Giants
New England Patriots	Washington Redskins
New York Jets	St. Louis Cardinals

Confused? Well, don't be. Someone once said that consistency is the mark of small minds, and rest assured, the men who run the NFL are anything but small-minded.

There is more to a division than geography. There is a style, a tone, an attitude that goes with it. The Central Division of the NFC has been called the "black and blue" division. The teams in this division are noted for "straight ahead" football. That is, give the ball to the biggest, baddest man in the backfield, charge the line forward, and let the ballcarrier pound his body into the resulting mishmash of arms, legs, helmets, and muscle. The impression is that the longest pass thrown by a NFC Central quarterback is something over six yards, and that in an extreme emergency. That myth lives on even though the facts are quite different. Perhaps it has something to do with a preconception of the Midwest, or perhaps it has to do with the weather. In November or December, the Detroit Lions or the Chicago Bears might be playing a game on a frozen, snow-covered field at 12°F., in a raging blizzard with the wind blowing forty five miles an hour directly from the North Pole via one of the Great Lakes. Simultaneously, the Rams or Chargers are romping around in the sun and smog with the palm trees swaying in a semitropical breeze.

Yet in that blizzard, a fifty-yard "bomb" is thrown, or a Gale Sayers slants his body to one side, slips a tackle, squirts through the tiniest hole, pivots on his hips, changes direction and runs with incredible grace for a thirty- or forty-yard touchdown. The man who raised broken field running to the level of a Baryshnikov dance recital played all his professional life for the Chicago Bears.

There is a beauty and grace to this game that goes unnoticed in the crash of bodies and the earth-shattering tackles. And when the contending lines smash into each other like two rows of bulldozers in a head-on collision, these are not machines but men smashing their muscle and gristle into one another. Muscles bruise and cartilage tears, and all men feel pain.

THE FIELD

Bullfighters perform veronicas and drag their muletas on the arena sands. The *arena* means *sand* in Spanish. Sand is a fine surface for bullfighting. It soaks up with equal efficiency the blood of the slain bull and that of the gored bullfighter. Just add a little from the nearest beach, rake it in, and presto! like new. All signs of battle gone. There are all sizes of arenas, but all football fields are the same size, 100 yards long (300 feet) by 53.333 yards wide (160 feet). The hundred yards seems reasonable; the 53.333 . . .? In any event, that's the way it is.

At each end of the one hundred yards, there is a ten-yard (thirty feet) end zone. At the back of each end zone, right smack dab on the line, is a strange, pagan-looking construction called the goalpost. It used to look like the letter H. Now it looks like a stylized Y with the upper V arms changed into a broad bottomed U. For those of you who don't know the alphabet or are completely confused by this description, see Figure 1, the goalposts.

The field is divided into 20 five-yard grid lines, usually by white chalk lines on the natural turf or white plastic stuff on the plastic grass (or artificial turf as it is euphemistically called). Along each of the sidelines the intervening one-yard

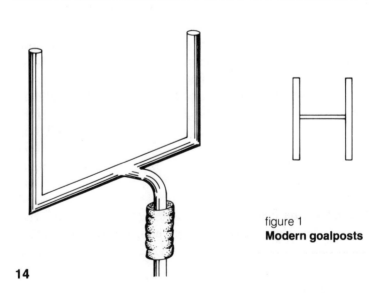

figure 1
Modern goalposts

14

lines are noted by short white markers. Seventy feet nine inches in toward the center from each of the sidelines, these one-yard markers are repeated. These are the hash marks. If you take 70 feet 9 inches from each sideline, that leaves 18 feet 6 inches between the hash marks in the middle of the field. If you have a visual mind rather than an arithmetical mind, look at Figure 2. That's what a football field looks like.

The lines are marked from the center in both directions toward the end zones. The center line is the 50-yard line. Two lines away (ten yards) are the 40-yard lines followed by the 30-yard lines and so forth. Down in front of the end zones, the 2-yard lines are specially marked. As you will learn later on, it is from these humble marks that the point-after-touchdown conversions are snapped. Many a game has been won or lost from these 2-yard marks.

The sidelines are more interesting than one would expect. They are six feet wide but the field starts from the *inside* of the line. If a player steps on the line but not outside it, he is still out of bounds. How many games are decided over a quarter of an inch one way or the other? And of course, you sometimes have to wonder at the official's visual acuity. The cliché "it's a game of inches" usually refers to where the ball is placed in its journeys up and down the field, but it could also apply to sidelines and encroaching "pedal extremities," as the late Fats Waller was wont to say. "Your Feets Too Big" could the theme song of many a coach.

Finally, there is one more landmark outside the sidelines, the bench. The bench is where the players who are not playing sit while waiting their turn on the field. The bench is also a psychological condition, a philosophical position, and the last resting place of those heroes who have battled their last battle, faced their last enemy, performed their last impossible feat of self-sacrifice for the cause. They sit, aged and grizzled, old warriors with aching knees and throbbing wounds, waiting for the moment each knows is coming. The

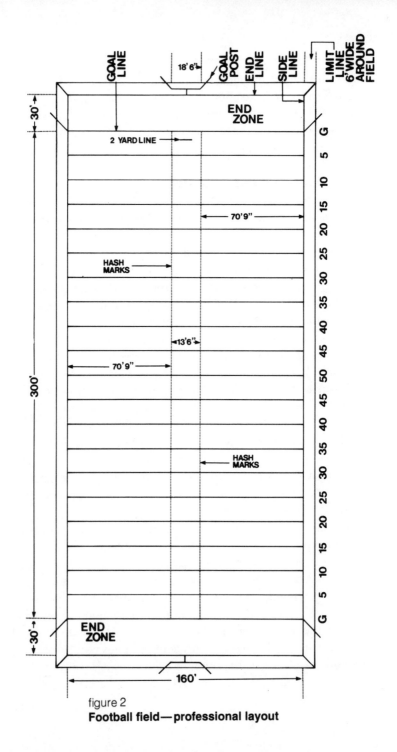

figure 2
Football field—professional layout

moment when the coach, frustrated by the childish antics of his immature first-stringers, turns to his veterans and says, "Men, I need a volunteer. I need someone who knows the territory to get in there and knock down that dashity-dash linebacker on the weak side over there, and spring loose our speedy running back." The linebacker in question is 22 years old, in perfect health, measures 6 feet 17 inches, weighs 280 pounds, runs the 40-yard dash in under 5 seconds, and hits like a Mack truck. The best the veteran can expect is four crushed ribs and a large bruise running from groin to clavicle. Does he hesitate? Does he worry if his Medicare account is in proper order? Does he go? Does he GO? He can't wait. To run out into the sunshine radiating from tens of thousands of hero worshippers and once more to put his gnarled knuckles on the freezing turf and stare eyeball to eyeball at his equal and opposite a few feet away is what he lives for. Next year, he could be selling insurance, but this year, he's an active pro-football player, and not just a bench-warmer either.

There is other paraphenalia along the sidelines; down markers, the chain, and so forth. We'll tell you about that stuff later on in this book. For now just know that they are there.

This is as good a time as any to get into a controversial subject, turf. Turf is the surface that football players play football on. Until the modern era of fake everything, from plastic flowers to nondairy creamer to wood-grained contact paper, grass used to be grass. It was green if sufficiently watered, grew in earth and required mowing. When you fell on it, two things happened: you got grass stains on your pants, and it was softer than rock so there was a slight cushioning effect. It was kind of nice to run on and, unless it was very wet, provided good springy traction. But grass has several drawbacks. It refuses to grow indoors, requires watering, must be mowed, and when it gets torn up by two armies, parts have to be replaced. All of those characteristics except the first cost money. Team owners and stadium operators, in common with other businessmen, hate to spend money, or at least they prefer to save money. So when an enclosed stadium was built in the oil capital of the great Southwest, Houston, and the grass wouldn't grow inside the dome, Astroturf™ was born. It grew without compunction inside an enclosed structure, never required water, never needed mowing, and required partial replacement only after the most unusual punishment. Since it had no life, it couldn't be killed.

Well, the economic scintillation of such a substance caught the eye of owners and operators everywhere. The plastic revolution was underway. At season's end, bulldozers were introduced to the gridiron and the offending grass was torn up, scraped off, the top soil piled up, trucked away, and the surface carefully graded. Crushed rock was deposited for a solid base and asphalt steamrollered on. Then rolls and rolls of plastic grass were laid out and sewn together something like wall-to-wall carpet. Voilà! Astroturf™ or Polyturf™ or what have you. Very even green with practically no variation in color or texture. Twenty less groundskeepers. No more chalk lines that faded and blurred. Let's play ball!

Then the injuries started. Running hard on an ungiving surface sent shock waves into the leg joints and along the spinal column. Friction burns from sliding exposed skin along the plastic grass left purplish raw places that didn't seem to heal all that quickly. And for some reason, the stuff wouldn't give when you tried to pivot fast. Bad ankle and knee injuries, separated shoulders and shortened career lives; those were the complaints of the players and their organizations.

There is still plenty of fake grass in the NFL, but the trend seems to be back to natural grass. And it is welcomed by everyone except the makers of Astroturf™ and Polyturf™ and their ilk. Of course, more and more cities are talking about covered stadiums and grass won't grow inside them, so fake hasn't lost yet.

WHO'S ON FIRST—THE POSITIONS

On the field two opposing teams of eleven men each face each other. Time was when each man had both an offensive and a defensive responsibility. Now each club fields three different teams. These are the *offense,* the *defense,* and *special teams.* The functions of the first two are obvious; the special teams appear on the field at kickoffs only. They do their thing and return to the sidelines. Special team members spend most of their waking hours dreaming about getting off the special team. Some actually make it.

The offense consists essentially of a line and a backfield. The line, or "forward wall," consists of the center, the right and left guards, and the right and left tackles. These are known as the interior linemen. Lining up close to the interior linemen and on the line of scrimmage are one or more ends (tight or split). The backfield consists of various backs. The backs, along with the ends, are the only players permitted to carry the ball or receive passes. There is always a quarterback and some combination of running backs, wide receivers, and a fullback. The problem with defining the backfield is that is changes from formation to formation and team to team. Depending on what is expedient (or sometimes who is left uninjured), the formation might be two tight ends, a wide receiver, two running backs and the quarterback. Other times, it might be two wide receivers and a fullback, one tight end and a halfback along with the quarterback.

The defense also consists of a line and players who line up off the line of scrimmage. There are many defensive sets, but the defensive line consists of three or four "down linemen," three or four linebackers, and the defensive backfield. Typically the defensive backfield consists of two cornerbacks and two safeties.

The special teams are the regular offensive and defensive teams with the following differences:

1. On the kicking side are the kicker and the special substitutes who go running like crazy to catch and bring down the masochist who is waiting to receive the ball.

2. On the receiving side, the special team consists of the aforementioned masochist and the substitutes who are supposed to protect him from the guys who are running like crazy to bring him down. Add to this mélange the placekicker (who may or may not be the same person as the kickoff kicker) and the punter (who also may or may not be one of the two above kickers). Confused? Well, so is the kicking game. For a game called *football,* there is not much kicking left anymore, but what there is is important enough to dedicate two or three people to foot the football. See Figure 3 for typical offensive and defensive formations. Remember that the variations are many and subtle.

What do all these people do? You'll have to wait until we get to the section on tactics, but bear one fact in mind. Some of these people aren't permitted to have anything to do with the ball unless somebody who does have the right to hold it, lets go. Then it's a free-for-all. Down linesmen have given their eyeteeth to get their taped hands on a football. With all that tape, however, they have the manual dexterity of a kitchen stove. The tape effectively welds their fingers and hands into crab claws. Yet they do sometimes grab the ball or tear off the quarterback's jersey.

The players all have both numbers and names lettered on their jerseys. The names identify the individuals and are usually inherited from their parents along with the physical and psychological attributes that made it possible to become professional football players in the first place. The numbers are thrust upon them by the rules of the National Football League. These rules designate certain blocks of numbers to particular positions and identify the players to the fans, coaches, the officials, and Howard Cosell (and you thought he was so smart that he knew the players by sight). The position numbers are:

1. quarterbacks including kickers—1 through 19
2. running and defensive backs—20 through 49
3. centers and linebackers—50 through 59
4. offensive guards, tackles, and their defensive counter- parts, the defensive linemen—60 through 79
5. wide receivers and tight ends—80 through 89

And, in the pre-season before the teams are cut to their allowable 44 players, numbers 90 and up are also used.

Now, when you see someone running like crazy down the field and you see that his number is 82, you turn to your husband, lover, wife, or mother-in-law and with a voice full of confidence say, "Oh, there goes that big tight end running a down and out pattern. I bet that number twelve, the quarterback, is going to throw him a forward pass." And very possibly he is.

THE OBJECT OF THE GAME

It may seem very obvious that the object of the game is to win, and that, of course, is true. But how does a team win? By scoring more points than the other team, that's how. How does a team score points? By—

1. scoring a touchdown—6 points
2. kicking a field goal—3 points

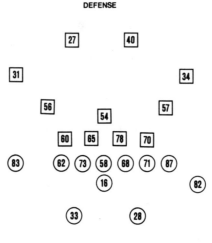

DEFENSE

OFFENSE

figure 3
**Typical offensive formation
and defensive alignment**

---

3. kicking a point-after-touchdown conversion (in theory the ball can also be run across the goal line)—1 point
4. inflicting a safety—2 points

A touchdown consists of—

1. carrying the ball across the vertical plane of the goal line, or
2. catching a forward pass while in the end zone, or
3. recovering an offensive team's fumble in their end zone, or
4. recovering a ball kicked into the end zone that has been touched by a member of the receiving team

Several words of explanation are in order here. "The vertical plane of the goal line" is an imaginary surface extending up to Heaven across the entire playing field from the *inside* of the sidelines. The goal line is the edge of the end zone

---

nearest the 1-yard line. If this imaginary "surface" is penetrated by a fraction of an inch the goal line has been crossed. Have a look again at Figure 2, the field diagram.

As to touchdown method number 4, you are not very likely to see that in NFL play. When the ball is kicked into the end zone, the receiving team scrambles for the ball the way ants rush into an open jar of grape jelly at the family picnic.

A field goal consists of kicking the ball across the plane of the goalpost crossbar. Like all vertical planes, it too extends up to Heaven, but its boundaries are the crossbar at the bottom and the uprights of the goalpost at the sides. To the best of our knowledge, no angel has yet been struck in full flight by an ascending pigskin. (Just to keep everything kosher, the pigskin is really cowhide.) To kick a field goal, the center "snaps" the ball from between his legs, back to the "holder" who puts it, point down, on the ground, and supports it in this position while the kicker runs his particular number of steps and kicks the ball toward Heaven in the direction of the vertical plane of the crossbar. This is worth three points.

A point-after-touchdown (PAT) conversion is similar in that we're interested in the same vertical plane over the crossbar. It is also snapped by the center to a holder and kicked from under his hand, but differs from a field goal in several respects. First, the team has to have just scored a touchdown before it can kick the PAT. The ball is snapped from the 2-yard line and, if successful, is worth one point. But don't sneeze at that one point. Many a game has been decided by the success or failure of a PAT.

A safety occurs when someone on the offense is tackled in his own end zone while in possession of the ball. That's worth two points of score and about eight hundred points of psychological advantage. The team that suffers a safety tends to feel a more than mild chagrin. Coaches consider it a personal insult and will occasionally utter epithets like "darn," "son-of-a-gun," and "mother fachamali." The gentle ears of the unfortunate player caught with the ball and slung to the turf in his own end zone, have been known to turn crimson at such unbridled language!

In order to score these points (except for the safety) a team must obtain and keep possession of the football; that is, be the offensive team. That leads us inexorably to another concept, *downs*. There are four of them: first down, second down, third down, and fourth down. A down can be thought of as an attempt to move the football. To maintain possession of the ball, the offensive team has four tries to move the ball at least ten yards. If the ball does get moved ten yards from where the first attempt has been started, this qualifies as a *first down* and they now have four more tries to get the next ten yards. If it doesn't go the ten yards, the other team gets possession. In practice, most of the time, if after the third attempt (third down) they haven't reached their required ten yards, the ball is punted (kicked) away to the other team. This is done by the special team. The ball is snapped by the center to the kicker directly (no holder), he holds it in front of him, drops it, and kicks it before it reaches the ground. The opposing team has one or more receivers downfield who catches it (hopefully) and runs the ball as far as he can. The kicking team tries their damnedest to knock him down as soon as they can. If the ball goes out of the sidelines before it gets to the end zone, untouched by anybody, the ball gets spotted on the yard line where it went out of bounds. If it goes into the end zone and then out of bounds, it is called a *touchback* and it is spotted on the 20-yard line. Similarly, if it is caught in the end zone and not run out, that too is a touchback. Another option is the *fair catch*. If the receiver signals for a fair catch, he has to catch the ball and not attempt to run it forward. In a fair catch, nobody can legally tackle the receiver. More on this in Chapter Seven. Lastly, if the ball is not caught or touched by a receiving player, stays inbounds, and does not go into the end zone, a kicking team player *grounds* (touches) the ball. Play starts from where he grounds the ball.

IT'S A MATTER OF TIME

There are three master clocks in all our lives, the revolution of the earth around the sun, the rotation of the earth around its axis, and the revolution of the moon around the earth. The first defines our year, the second defines our days and nights, and the third defines our tides, months, and various biological cycles. The earth revolves around the sun in 364 and a fraction days; the earth rotates around its axis in 24 hours; the moon manages to come around the earth in about 25 hours. Football is played in one hour of playing time. And there lies the basic difference between a game and "real" life. In real life, time is inexorable. When twenty four hours is up you can't say, "wait another five minutes, I'm not quite finished." At one instant beyond midnight, it's tomorrow whether you like it or not. In football, however, there is the *time-out*, which stops the clock, *stepping out* or *throwing out* of bounds, which stops the clock, and the *incomplete pass*, which also stops the clock. Sometimes the last two minutes of play take ten or fifteen minutes. Einstein was right. Time is relative and variable.

All that aside, the sixty minutes of playing time are broken into 15-minute quarters with a break in the action between the second and third quarter. That makes it something like two separate games, the first half and second half. The only difference is that after the first half, you get a second chance. After the second half, you don't. Unless you tie, it's all over.

There are actually two clocks in a football game. There is the official game clock, the one on the scoreboard, and there is the thirty-second clock, also on the scoreboard. The thirty-second clock monitors the time it takes to get off the play. It starts when an official signals the start of play and it runs for thirty seconds. In that time, the offense has to huddle, line up, shift, tie its individual shoelaces, wipe its individual noses, take on its "I ain't afraid of you, so you better be afraid of me" look, call signals, and get off the play. Getting off the play means snapping the ball. If all this takes more than thirty seconds, the referee blows his whistle, folds his arms as if in disgust, and points his finger accusingly at the offending team. "Delay of game—offense—five-yard penalty." Everybody moves the five yards, and they start the thirty-second clock all over again.

While this is going on, the game clock may or may not be running, depending on how the preceding play terminated. If the game clock had been stopped, it starts again when the ball is snapped. The rules on stopping the game clock are as follows:

1. Time-out is called by either the offensive or defensive team captain. No one else on either team can call a time-out. This time-out lasts two minutes and is charged against the calling team. Each team has only three time-outs per half. It pays to hoard these for the last two minutes of play.

2. Someone carrying the ball steps out of bounds. He can do this on his own volition or be pushed out by the defense.

3. An incomplete pass.

4. An infraction of the rules, seen and called by an official. Like life in the big city, you can break laws, but there are no penalties unless someone catches you.

5. After a score. Any score will do, touchdown, field goal, safety.

6. After a free kick; that is, a kickoff. There is one other kind of free kick, but it is such a rarity that to all intents and purposes it can be ignored in this section.

7. At the referee's discretion. He blows his whistle and, like the deity he is, time stops. Most usually, he does this in the event of an injury to a player on the field.

8. To permit time for a TV commercial. Now this practice has been denied, but . . .

Please note that a PAT conversion does not affect the clock.

As described, a time-out stops the clock for two minutes; however, the thirty-second clock starts after one-and-a-half minutes and the offensive team must get off the play within that two minutes.

At the end of each quarter, the teams are given two minutes to switch positions on the field, because the goal switches ends of the field at the end of each quarter. The team that was defending the east goal switches and defends the west goal—and vice versa.

At the end of the first half there is a fifteen-minute halftime period, during which both teams leave the field and go to the locker room where actor Pat O'Brien tells them to win one for the Gipper, played by the President of the United States. After a rousing Yale fight song and a shot of amphetamines mixed with procaine and vitamin C, our warriors are ready for the second half. Actually, we don't have the slightest idea of what really goes on in the locker room at halftime. Probably there is a lot of retaping and bruise medicating, equipment adjustments, and discussions on second-half tactics based on the first-half experiences. Then there has to be time to rest. All that hitting and running, throwing and catching is hard work.

In the last two minutes of play for each half, something curious happens. Tension, always present in a football game, starts to build. This is especially true if the score is close. In some cases, the tension approaches the unbearable. Down on the field, the players with the most experience, the coolest by nature, the real pros, are doing their thing, The *two-minute drill*, practiced to hopeful perfection, is pulled out and applied by the offense. The defense has its own two-minute game, the *prevent defense*.

The two-minute drill consists of getting off as many plays within the two minutes as possible. It consists of purposely passing the ball incomplete or out of bounds to stop the clock. The officials rarely call a penalty for *intentional grounding* if there is the slightest pretense of a would-be receiver on which to hang the rationale. Several plays are called in the huddle and the subsequent plays start without the time-consuming huddles. If there is no other way to stop the clock, they reluctantly call a time-out. Remember, there are only three. They must be hoarded and doled out only when there is no alternative. Depending on the score differential, the offense could opt to get within field goal range, run the clock down to its last remaining seconds, and then kick for the three-pointer. This is done if either three points are enough to win the game, or three are enough points to put the game out of reach for the opposition, even if they had time to run the plays. For example, suppose team A on offense was behind by one point, a missed PAT. They play conservative ball-control football to minimize any chance of a turnover and fight their way to, say, the 35-yard line of team B, wasting as much time as possible. They call a time-out with seven seconds left (often it might be only one second left), and stop the clock. The field goal kicker comes running on the field. The sweat in his armpits has turned to icicles. The whole game, perhaps the whole season, conceivably his entire career, is riding on this kick. The ball is snapped, caught, and set. He takes his three or four steps and the ball is up and—over? or off to one side? or blocked?

The defense has its *prevent defense.* Also dependent on the score, they will try (1) to stop the offense without any chance of scoring (always a defensive task); (2) to get the ball and run it back the other way for a turnover, or better yet, a score; or (3) to keep the offense from scoring enough points to win. For example, if the offense needs six or seven points to win, it may be all right to give them the short yardage and let the clock run down, but protect against the long ball with its attendant touchdown possibilities.

Playing the clock has its subtleties.

ARMOR

Armor is the equipment football players wear to protect themselves as the knights of old wore chain mail at their tournaments. The equipment is what makes a normal sized (well, normally large sized) man look like a hulking giant from our Neanderthal past. Huge shoulders tapering down to narrow waists make fantastically macho photographs. Football players spend a lot of time in front of some of the most expensive optics in the world. Very flattering.

But the reason is not cosmetic, it's protective. The league requires a minimum set of protective equipment in addition to its uniform requirements. The league's requirements are simplicity itself. All you need on your body to be legal is a helmet, a jersey with a number on it, football pants, and socks. You aren't even required to wear shoes. Thus the barefooted kicker is perfectly legal. In a recent playoff game in Philadelphia, with the ground frozen, the temperature at about 8°F. and a wind chill factor of −17°, the placekicker limped out on the field with one foot bare. Kicked a field goal, too. That same season, in a crucial situation, one player in a nationally televised game was penalized for droopy socks. If you don't believe it, look it up in one of the football trivia books.

The rest of the rules tell the players what they can't wear. They can't wear aluminum cleats, plastic face guards, or detachable kicking toes. We don't know what a detachable kicking toe is, but it's a fascinating idea. Imagine, the kicker comes out to punch the ball over the uprights for a three-point field goal. As he swings his foot, the entire front end of his shoe flies off two full steps before the kicker gets there. This would completely confuse the kick blockers of the defense, who, not realizing that the ball has already been kicked, rough the kicker for an additional fifteen yards to be tacked onto the beginning of the next play.

The players are completely free to wear athletic supporters (point of vanity with some of them, no doubt), T-shirts, with or without little ditties printed on them, any other kind of underwear they want, and unlimited quantities of white adhesive tape. Some players have so much tape on their bodies they require a subsidy from Johnson and Johnson. The tape is usually applied to the vulnerable parts of the human anatomy, the ankles, wrists, back, ribs, thighs, and forearms. The only thing that has never been taped in professional football history is the teeth. And that's only because it's hard to get the stuff to stick on teeth.

Forearms on linemen of both persuasions get a lot of tape for support because they are used as battering rams and require a lot of stiffening.

Pads of all descriptions are used and are legal. These include hip pads, knees pads, elbow pads, rib pads, shin pads, shoulder pads, wrist pads, and some pads whose application locations are not for the gentle ears nor eyes of the general public.

In recent years, some new equipment has been coming into vogue. Inflatable pads are being worn more and more, especially to protect an already injured area. The future holds even more protective devices as the injuries mount up and the public shows some concern.

2

Tactics

Tactics are all the little squares and circles of Figure 3 with lines and arrows showing who goes where, when, for what reason, to do this or that and the other thing. Coaches visualize things in vector terms, all diagramed with direction and velocity. All these diagrams get bound together to form a secret document called the playbook, which the players study and are tested on. Players get fined if they fail, and losing a playbook is a crime akin to treason. There are security agents and spies; espionage agents and counterespionage agents engaged in stealing the secret and safeguarding it, respectively. And just as soon as there is a trade of players between clubs, the secret is out.

In reality, there aren't any secrets, at least not for long. Once a team executes a double whammy quadruple reverse, with the tight end "dishing off" to the fullback, who then reverses his field and laterals back to the quarterback, who in turn throws a screen pass to the other back, who has run a buttonhook pattern and is finally tackled after a gain of four yards, that play is no longer a secret. It is on film and will be carefully analysed. No detail is too trivial. The films will be studied for the eye movements of the quarterback, tight end, fullback, running back, offensive coach, and the pretty brunette cheerleader doing the bump and grind near the $35 seats. The next time that play is used, the defense trots out its patented noncarborundum illigitimatum anti-quadruple reverse defense and it's all over.

The point of this mumbo jumbo is that there are basic football moves the offense can make and these can be countered by basic moves the defense can make. The offense never has more than three options. They can run the football. They can pass the football. They can kick the football. Very often what they do is a combination of the first two. Kicking is usually a tactic used when the first two fail to produce a first down or a touchdown. The defense has its own options, but in the final analysis their job is to contain the territorial ambitions of the offense. "Thou shalt not give up yardage" is the basic commandment of the defensive team. Football is the game version of the Territorial Imperative.

OFFENSIVE TACTICS

An offensive football play starts from a formation. There are many formations, each of which has been planned to obtain a particular result. Some are designed to facilitate a pass, some to facilitate a run. Others provide the quarterback with an option; ie., to pass or run, depending on the way the play develops. Each formation is called an offensive *set*.

A typical professional formation is the *open set*, shown in Figure 4. The open set uses a seven-man line with a split end to one side and a tight end to the other. A flankerback positions himself wide and behind the tight end. The quarterback gets right behind the center and the two running

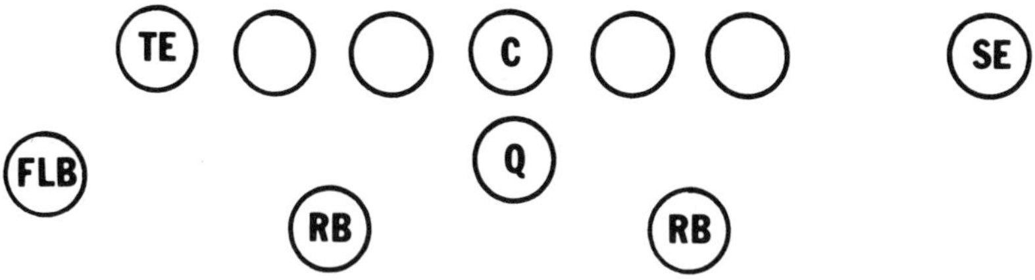

figure 4
Open set

backs usually place themselves on either side of him about four yards farther back. They line up behind the space between their guards and tackles. The split end and tight end can be on either side of the line depending on the direction the play is designed to go.

The strength of the open set is its versatility. The defense has to worry about the split end and the tight end going out as wide receivers. The pass is always a probability from this set. At the same time, there are two running backs ready to take a handoff and run through a hole in the line.

On the other hand, like every formation, it has its weaknesses. With only two runners in the backfield, it is hard to get enough blocking forward to open a hole in the line for a straight-ahead plunge.

A typical running play from the open set is a *slant off-tackle*. This is shown in Figure 5. On a slant off-tackle the ball is "snapped" to the quarterback on his signal. He takes it from between the center's legs, whirls around (to his left in our illustration) and jams it into the stomach of the running back who is crossing behind him. The running back now heads for the place between his left tackle and tight end. Theoretically, the tight end is blocking out the defensive end and the left tackle is blocking out the defensive tackle.

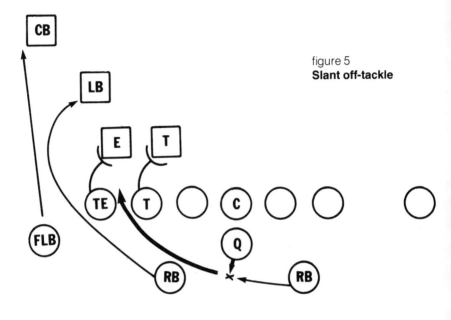

figure 5
Slant off-tackle

Meanwhile, the other running back, who apparently has nothing to do, runs like the devil to get between the linebacker and the ball carrier. The flankerback tries to look like he is going out to receive a pass and hopefully attract the attention of the defending cornerback. When this works, the ballcarrier bursts through the hole between the tackle and tight end for a significant gain.

A *line buck* is a similar play except that the running back tries to squirt through the space between the center and guard. That particular place is the stomping ground of the middle linebacker. It's usually used when the offense is in a short yardage situation. A diagram of the line buck is given in Figure 6.

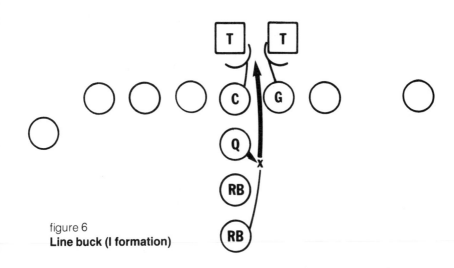

figure 6
Line buck (I formation)

A pretty sort of play, when it is successful, is the *draw*. Its chief characteristic is deception. In this play, diagramed in Figure 7, the offense tries to fool the defense into thinking that the play is going to be pass. When the ball is snapped, the quarterback drops back as if to pass. The linemen pretend they are little old ladies just waiting to get back to their knitting. The defensive players come roaring in to get the quarterback, but he doesn't even have the ball. The running back has filched it and is running past the quarterback-bound defensive players, heading for glory or at least a few yards. Unless they've read the play. It takes an optimist to play running back.

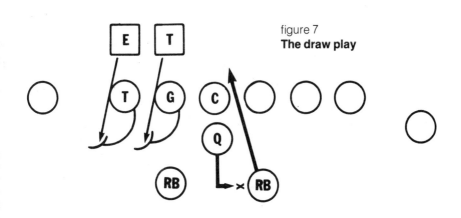

figure 7
The draw play

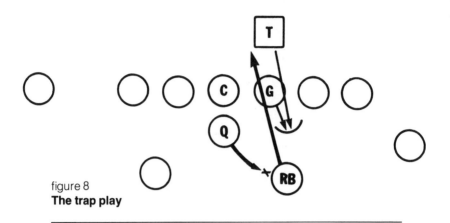

figure 8
The trap play

A *trap* is similar to a draw, also involving deception. The trap is executed by permitting the defender to break through into the backfield and then blocking him to one side. In theory, this leaves an avenue for the running back to get a big gain. Look at Figure 8 for a diagram of the trap.

All of the plays described so far are runs to the middle of the field. Some running plays are designed to permit the ballcarrier to run around the bulk of the defenders. If you are the offensive play caller and you have a very speedy, strong running back, you give him the ball and tell him to run like hell around the end of the defending team. One version is called the *sweep*. (Figure 9)

They used to call the sweep the *end run*, and some people still do. The basic advantage of the sweep is momentum. The runner whips past the quarterback after the snap. The quarterback pivots and jams the ball into the running back's belly while his is building up speed. The fullback and both guards run interference toward the side the sweep is going. When the running back is past the last defender still left standing by the blockers, he "turns the corner"; that is, he turns up the field and runs as fast as his little legs will carry him. The guy he has to look out for is not the Big Bad Wolf, but the big bad linebacker and his cohorts, the smaller but badder cornerback and still badder safety. These gentlemen of

36

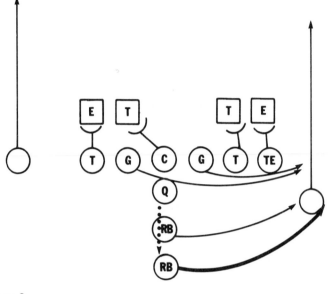

figure 9
The sweep play (I formation)

---

refinement are apt to throw their considerable bulk at the running back with total disregard of the laws of physics. The law they disregard the most is the one about two bodies occupying the same space.

The sweep is a power play. No deception. Add deception to the end run and you have the *end around reverse*. This little gem starts out looking for all the world like a power sweep, but the split end comes dashing over in the opposite direction, grabs the ball from the quarterback, and continues to run "against the grain." The key to success in this play is the fullback, who must a great method actor. When he makes believe he has the ball, he believes it and hopefully so do the defenders. They chase after him and our sly fox, the

---

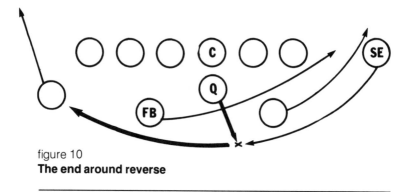

figure 10
The end around reverse

split end, is in the clear. The whole story is told in the diagram of Figure 10.

Tricky as the end around reverse may be, it can get trickier. You could have a double reverse or a triple reverse. We will diagram the double reverse, but the triple reverse is too complicated and requires too many arrows and stuff. Besides, we don't approve of *that* much trickiness.

You can see what happens in a double reverse. The quarterback runs to his right and hands the ball to the wingback, who runs to his left. He gives the ball to the running back, who runs the ball back to the right. The object of all this right-left-right is to reduce the defense to a mass of quivering jelly so wracked with indecision and confusion that they

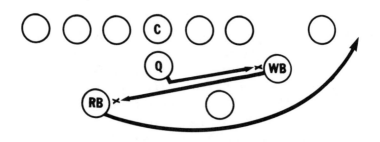

figure 11
The double reverse

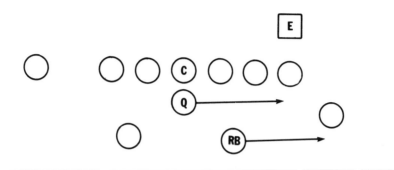

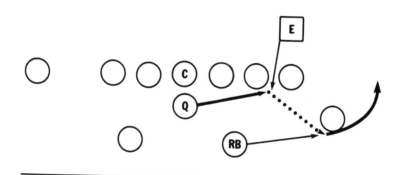

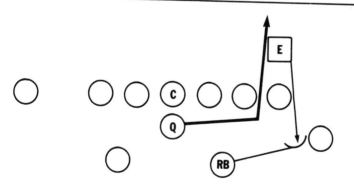

figure 12
The quarterback option

stop, take off their helmets and scratch their heads in unison. When this happens the offense makes a big gain.

A play you see once in a while in the professional game (although fairly commonly at the college level) is the *quarterback option*. With a strong, young quarterback whose knees haven't yet been welded open by repeated surgery, the quarterback option is a very effective play. It permits the quarterback to either keep the ball and run it himself, or if things go badly, pitch it out to a running back. Its strength lies in the fact that he doesn't have to make up his mind until the defense has committed itself. At least, that's the theory.

Here's how it works. The ball is snapped to the quarterback. He heads toward one of the defensive ends. About five yards behind him, a running back is on a parallel course. The quarterback keeps his eyes fixed on the defensive end.

If the defensive end tears a hole in the forward wall and, with murder in his heart, aims his body and arms at the ballcarrier, the quarterback tosses the ball to the running back, who goes around him for a large gain down the sidelines.

If the defensive end decides that the quarterback is not going to carry the ball himself, he might head toward the running back instead. In that event, the quarterback does *not* toss the ball behind him, but runs the ball himself. The three-part diagram of Figure 12 shows the progression of events.

An even more interesting version of the option play is the triple option. In the triple option, our hero has one more thing he can do, depending on what the defense does. The diagram of Figure 13 shows the triple option as executed from a formation known as the wishbone-T. It's called that because the fullback lines up directly behind the quarterback with both running backs behind and to both sides of the fullback.

In this play the quarterback takes the handoff from the

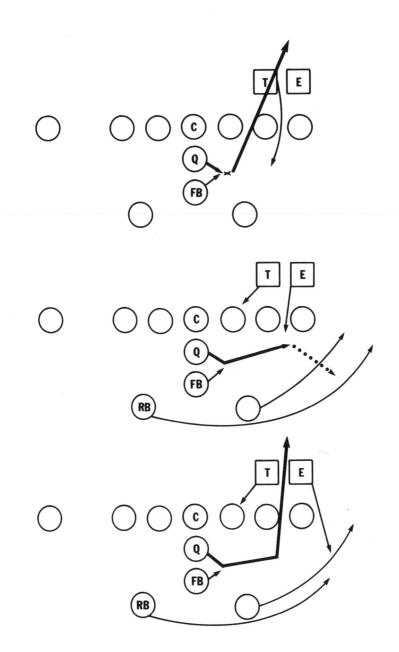

figure 13
The triple option

center and drops back as if to hand off to the fullback. He keeps his eyes on the defensive tackle on the side to which the play will run. If the defensive tackle charges the quarterback, he can indeed give the ball to the fullback, who runs toward the area vacated by the onrushing tackle.

If the defensive tackle heads for the fullback instead, the quarterback keeps the ball and runs toward the vacated area. The running back now parallels him about five yards back. This gives the quarterback the option of tossing the ball to the running back if necessary.

These are some of the running plays possible. There are others with a large number of variations. If the threat of a forward pass is added, the situation becomes even more dynamic.

The passing game is a gamble. Woody Hayes, when head coach of Ohio State, once said, "When you throw a forward pass, there are only three things that can happen, and two of them are bad." Needless to say, his teams were not noted for their passing brilliance. The point however, is well taken. When the ball is put into the air, there are only three possibilities:

1. the ball will be caught by an offensive receiver
2. the ball will not be caught by anyone
3. the ball will caught by a defensive player.

That last one, the interception, is bad news for the offense because, in addition to blunting the attack, it turns the ball over to the opposition.

Like most gambles, when the forward pass works, it usually picks up significant yardage, often enough for a touchdown. It is also very exciting to watch. The passer, usually the quarterback, takes the handoff, drops back, and throws it. Just watching the ball is somehow uplifting. The trajectory is parabolic, that is, a beautifully curved path through the air—from the quarterback's flashing arm, up and over the pedestrians on the field, spiraling to the hands of the receiver who is running at full speed. It is as if fate decrees that the ball and the man arrive at the same spot at the same time. Interestingly, the parabola is one of the most pleasing curves found in nature. It is the shape of the underside of a woman's breast, the mathematical description of the natural cycles of sunrise and sunset, the seasons, of life itself. When the ball goes up, our hearts go with it, and when it is caught, there is a subliminal sigh of relief.

The forward pass looks simple enough, but looks can be deceiving. A successful pass results from a combination of precision, good strategy, athletic prowess, and a healthy element of good luck. In many ways, that last ingredient is the most important. Without a little luck, the team might just as well quit for the day and go shoot marbles for beers in the locker room. Good teams make their own luck.

Assuming that a quarterback has a good arm, can see over the defenders, and is blessed with undistorted vision, the most important requirement for a good passing game is an offensive line that gives him enough time to spot his receiver and throw the ball. The next most important element is the ability of the receiver(s) to "run a route" and get "open." In other words, to get where the ball is supposed to arrive and be free of defenders when he gets there. When all those things work, you have a successful forward pass. When they don't, you have a wasted down, or even worse, an interception. The look on the face of a passer who sees the opposition cornerback running toward him, cradling the ball meant for the wide receiver, brings back memories of a movie audience watching Camille expiring on her bed of pain. Makes you want to cry.

Let's look at these elements in reverse order, since the game on the line will be described later on in this section.

Who can legally catch a pass? The rules say that anyone

who plays in the backfield is eligible to catch a pass. That even includes the quarterback if he can get someone to throw one to him. It's not legal to catch your own pass. (It might make an interesting play, though, as the quarterback takes the handoff, drops back, throws a "bomb," and runs out to catch it. We could call it the Marx Brothers play.) In addition to the backs being eligible receivers, the ends, tight or split, are allowed to catch the ball. That's it. Everyone else is ineligible.

So, do all these eligible receivers go running out waving their arms crying, "Me, me. Throw it to me. I'm open. Hey, you dumbbell, can't you see I'm open ?" No, they run routes. Everything is timed so that the receiver is at the right spot at the right time. Very often, the passer throws to a spot on the field on a particular count. The receiver is also counting. Unless one of them is counting by ones while the other is counting by fives, the ball and the receiver should be in synch. That's the way is works in practice. Of course, when they're playing for real, a defensive player is busy harassing the receiver during the first five yards beyond the line of scrimmage. That's called "bump and run." Sounds like a dance out of the forties, doesn't it? If the defender is persistent, the receiver's timing is upset and, conceivably, the ball gets there before the runner does. When that happens, the TV commentator makes the remark, "Mel Kwabatinsky is a great quarterback, but this time, he just overthrew his receiver."

A *sideline pattern* is one of the good solid routes that usually picks up five or six yards when the running game is stymied. Here's how this one works. At the snap of the ball, the quarterback drops back a few yards, (about eight yards on a shallow drop, typically) and checks out the flankerback. That worthy gentleman sprints downfield about eight yards. He is going fast, so the defender in the secondary (defensive backfield) is convinced that the flankerback is going deep.

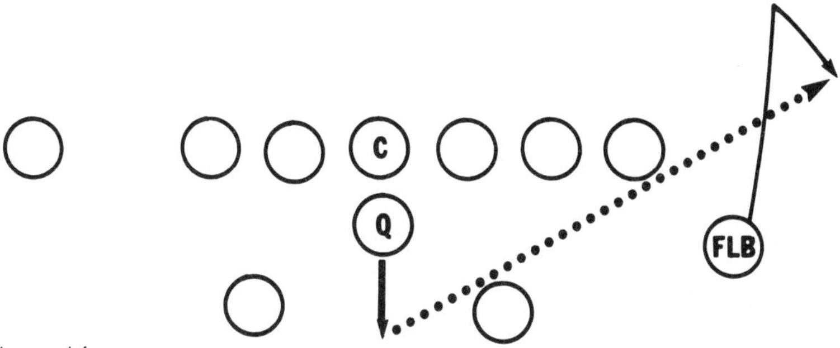

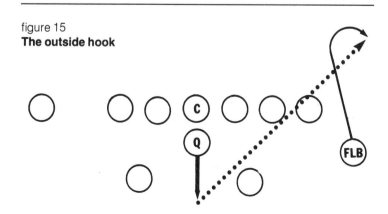

figure 14
The sideline pattern

The receiver, once he has faked out the defender, screeches to a halt and, planting his inside foot, pivots toward the outside. He comes back another two yards to make sure the defender is behind him and, if everyone's timing is right, catches the ball. Then, if he has any instincts for survival, he steps out of bounds. Of course, if the defender is till running in the wrong direction, the receiver will stay inbounds and run toward the goal line. As far as the timing is concerned, the quarterback must throw when the receiver plants that inside foot. If he waits until the receiver is at the catching position, it will be too late. What happens then is the quarterback is sacked (tackled, knocked down) because the offensive line probably can't contain the defense that long, or the defender who has run a few yards downfield has enough time to come back and break up the play. A diagram of the sideline pattern is given in Figure 14.

figure 15
The outside hook

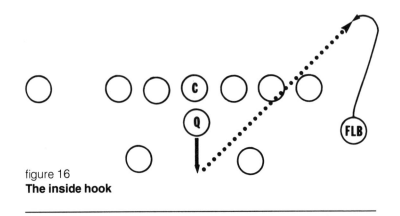

figure 16
The inside hook

The *hook pattern* is also a nice way to pick up that crucial seven or eight yards. There are essentially two versions of the hook. The *outside hook* is diagrammed in Figure 15 and the *inside hook* in Figure 16. The object in both cases is to drive the defensive coverage in one direction, then hook off to the other direction in time to catch the ball. The requirement here is that the receiver has to have the physical skills to stop and change direction quickly. On a wet or slippery field, making those sharp cuts is difficult. Receivers fall down, over run their pivot points, or concentrate so much on their footing that they lose the count. On the other hand, the defensive secondary is also slip-sliding around, which helps even things out.

One way to beat the defense is to be faster than they are, and one of the quickest pass patterns is the *slant*. Like the hook, there is a *slant out* and a *slant in*. These are shown in

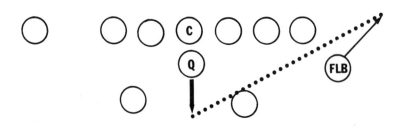

figure 17
Slant-out

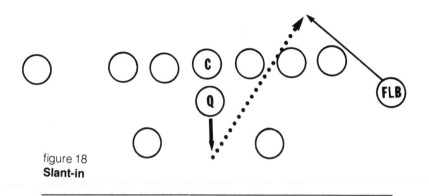

figure 18
Slant-in

Figures 17 and 18 respectively. When the ball is snapped, the receiver sprints at a 45-degree angle to the outside (or inside if it's a slant in). The quarterback takes two or three steps back and rifles the ball. These plays usually pick up short yardage, but occasionally the play develops so fast that it takes the defense by surprise and a substantial gain can be made. Sometimes the ball is thrown so hard it bounces off the catcher's hands like a flat pebble off a still pond. If one of the "bad guys" is there and catches it, it can be a costly "turnover." To avoid that kind of situation, quarterbacks are taught to throw the ball low. If the receiver can get the ball, fine. If he can't, it will probably become an incompleted pass.

There are variations of all these basic pass patterns. Sometimes, a team will run two receivers on opposite sides of the field. This gives the passer an option. It also serves to confuse the defense. Sometimes, if the play hasn't been practised enough, it confuses the offense. What it does to the officials is totally unknown. You will never see an official admit in any way that he doesn't know what's going on.

Another way to accomplish the same result as a slant is to run (1) *down-and-out,* (2) *down-and-in,* or (3) both simultaneously. What that last one looks like is shown in Figure

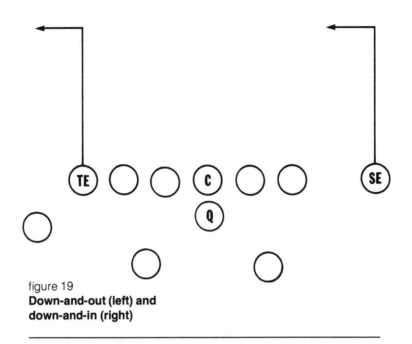

figure 19
**Down-and-out (left) and
down-and-in (right)**

19. In a down-and-out, the receiver-to-be, often a tight end, runs straight downfield, eluding his tormentors for about ten yards or so. Then, just when he has convinced everyone that he is running out for a long one, he cuts 90 degrees and runs toward the sidelines. The quarterback has dropped back and thrown the ball. If the timing is right, it can be a good gainer. Tight ends make a living driving defenders crazy trying to decide if it's going to be a long one or a down-and-out. It is most important that both the passer and receiver agree that it is going to be down-and-out. If they don't get it right, the tight end runs a down-and-out and the passer throws a long one downfield.

The down-and-in is similar. In this one, the split end runs straight downfield for his ten yards, and having driven off the defender, who is busy keeping himself between the receiver and the goal line, the split end does a 90-degree turn in toward the center. The quarterback whips him a short, hard pass and it's a first down. The quarterback has the option of throwing to whichever of the ends appears to be in the best position to catch the ball and get the biggest gain. The diagram in Figure 19 shows a simultaneous *down-and-out* and *down-and-in*.

So far, we've been describing the short bread-and-butter passes. They build up great passing statistics for the quarterback and are very useful when contract negotiation time comes around. Tactically, they tend to open up the defense. It's very hard to defense those short gainers. The cornerbacks and safeties are often willing to give up the short yards rather than take a chance of getting beaten on the long passes. So they "play off" a little, that is, don't drape themselves all over the receivers and stay between the receiver and the goal. If you watch closely, you will notice that a lot of the tackling on these short gainers is by the linebackers. The cornerbacks are guarding the corners and the safeties and hanging back protecting the rear. If a linebacker misses his man, the safety is ready to pop him one with his shoulder.

The longer passes are the nice ones to watch. Here's one that some people call the *flag route*. This is not a patriotic display—the flag in question marks the corner of the end zone, where the touchdowns live. Now we're getting into the "bomb" area, the long dramatic passes that lift the viewers out of their seats and make them gasp. Here is where the flashy receivers do their stuff, fake out and beat the defenders, catch the ball on a dead run and lope into the end zone. Conversely, here is where the fancy interceptions take place. Once the ball is up in the air, the defenders have as much right to catch it as the receivers do.

The standard basic *flag route* is shown in Figure 20. To make this pattern work, the wide receiver (or whoever is running it) has to beat the defender, that is, get out in front of him. The wide receiver gets off the line as fast as he can, takes his licks within the prescribed five yards, and runs

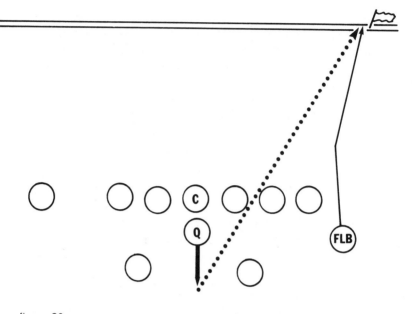

figure 20
The flag pattern

deceptively slowly through the secondary. By deceptively slowly, we mean at about three-quarters speed, which tends to make the defender suspicious. Here is this gazelle who can run the hundred yards in 9.3 seconds, idling around like your Aunt Tillie on the first day of her jogging regimen to lose sixty-five pounds. "Oh dear, whatever can this mean?" the defender thinks to himself. Can it be an attempt to "clear out" the defenders from a particluar area? (To attract attention and pull the defensive secondary toward the runner to leave someone else open.) Could it mean that the wide receiver is not really going to get a pass and so he isn't running his fool head off? Why waste all that energy if they're not throwing his way, anyhow. A little hesitation, that's what the wide receiver is looking for. A hint of uncertainty on the part of the pass defender(s). The wide receiver, having sneaked past the defender, cuts in to further confuse things, then cuts back out and runs toward the corner flag marking the end zone. Hopefully, the quarterback has already thrown the ball toward that very place. Our surehanded runner, going at his 9.3 speed now, has left the hapless defender puffing and sweating somewhere upfield. He gets to the designated spot as the ball does and TOUCHDOWN! The cheers are almost palpable. His teammates pound him on the head, back, and behind, pummeling him more than the defense has all day. The cheerleaders shake their pompons and various other protrusions. It's the stuff dreams are made of, and it really happens.

As usual there are variations on the theme, such as the *sideline flag* route shown in Figure 21. This looks like a short

figure 21
The sideline flag pattern

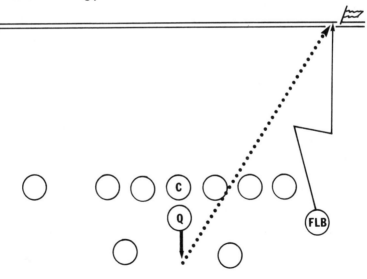

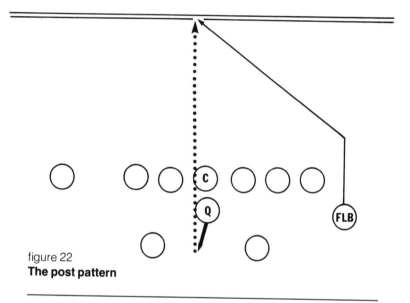

figure 22
The post pattern

sideline route and then, after the cut toward the sideline, the receiver runs like hell to the flag. The quarterback may even fake a pass toward the sideline and then throw long. Anything to help the runner pick up a step or two on his opposition helps; that and accuracy, and timing, and protection, and good luck.

Anyone who ever watched a professional football game on TV has heard someone mention the *post pattern* (Figure 22). Here's what that is. It looks like a flag pattern, but the receiver changes his direction and heads for the goalposts instead of the flag. Simple when you know, huh?

There are other passes designed primarily for receivers out of the backfield. These are the *screen pass*, the *flare*, and the *look-in*. The screen pass looks like a developing run. The idea is to draw the defenders in. To them it looks like a broken play. It's pig heaven for the defense. The quarterback looks trapped and is running for his life. Once the

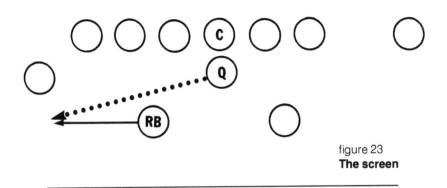

figure 23
The screen

defense has committed itself, the quarterback passes off to the side. If the offensive line plays it correctly and deceives the defense, it is very effective. The offensive tackle and guard fall back as if to block a running play on one side of the line. The receiver-to-be pretends to block and then takes off to the outside but still behind the line of scrimmage. The quarterback drops way back, looking for all the world like he is going to be sacked. The defensive types can smell his fear. That enrages them and they come charging in. They're committed. Meanwhile, the receiver has dropped his pretense of blocking. Nobody is looking at him anymore. Their attention is on the quarterback, who is running for his life. The receiver gets behind a screen of the end guard and tackle (hence the name *screen pass*) and catches the pass thrown by the quarterback an instant before he is knocked down (often, but not always). The screen then sets up a series of blockers in front of the ball carrier and it's off to the races. The diagram for the screen pass is Figure 23.

The flare is similar. The basic differences are that the

figure 24 **The flare**

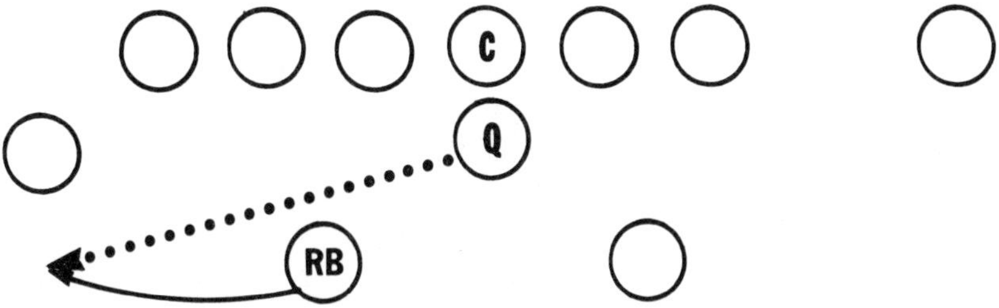

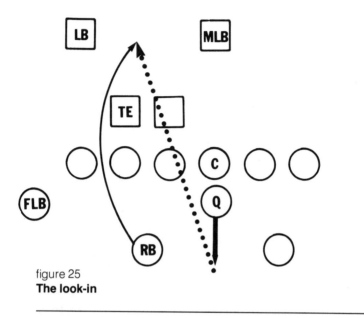

figure 25
The look-in

receiver makes (1) no attempt at deception, merely running to the point of reception in a "flare," a sort of curving path, and (2) attempts that the ball is thrown almost immediately. This one is a quick job, thrown very soon after the snap and usually for short yardage, rarely over five yards. Figure 24 shows the flare.

The *look-in* is a little different. The receiver squirts between the tight end and tackle and turns slightly toward the middle. The quarterback drops back a few yards and throws over the middle. From then on, if the ball is caught, the ballcarrier heads away from the opposition at an angle. See Figure 25 for a diagram.

Many pass plays use two or three receivers running different routes in an attempt to clear out the defenders so as to break one of them free. The quarterback has to spot the free man and make his play. Typical of these patterns are the

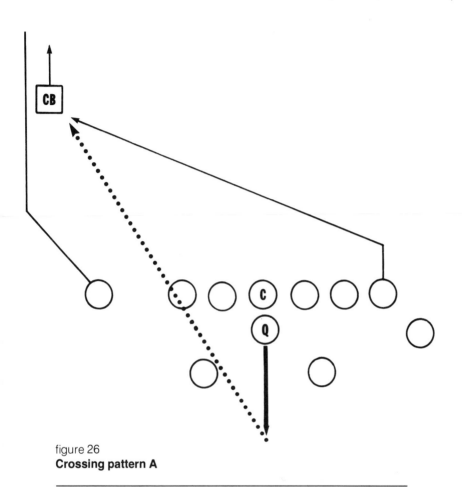

figure 26
Crossing pattern A

---

crossing patterns. One version of a crossing pattern uses the ends as receivers. Figure 26 shows the split end charging with all his strength and speed along the sideline at the snap of the ball. By now the cornerback has spotted him and thinks he is the primary receiver. As soon as the cornerback commits himself to defensing the split end, the tight end runs to the area vacated by the first cornerback and waits to catch the ball.

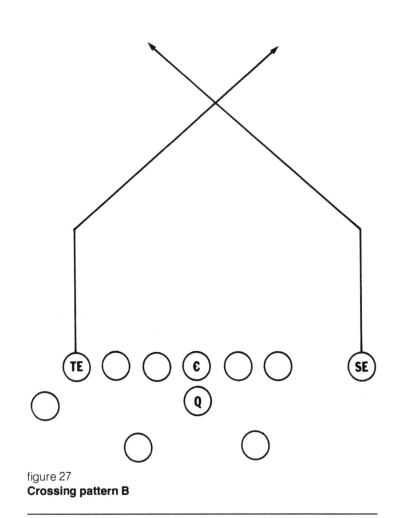

figure 27
Crossing pattern B

A different crossing pattern moves the ends downfield and across each other's routes. Whoever appears to be free becomes the receiver.

Another favorite play seen every Sunday and Monday night during the professional football season is the one you hear Mr. Cosell pontificate over: "If there is one play that the G-R-R-EAT coach of this G-R-R-E-A-T team, with its very, very, talented quarterback, knows how to execute, and gentlemen, that is what the name of this game we call professional football is all about, execution, it's that very exciting, very tricky, very difficult to stop play when it is executed the way this team can execute, and gentlemen, you know what I'm talking about . . . yes, I'm talking about the *play action pass*. Now, Dandy and What's-his-name, this play. . . ."

Let's talk about the play action pass. Mr. Cosell is not wrong, only a bit wordy. The play action pass is a running

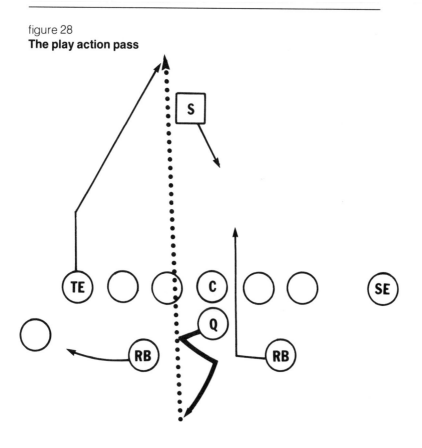

figure 28
The play action pass

play that ends up as a pass. It can start from just about any running play in the repertoire of the team. A typical play action pass might go something like this: The quarterback takes the handoff and fakes a flip to a running back. The running back jams himself into the line. The quarterback hides the ball along his thigh or behind his hip. He drops back to his passing position in the "pocket." The tight end takes off downfield. He might run straight at the defensive safety as if to block him. The safety says to himself, "Okay, buster, you want to play physical, I'll physical you." He prepares to tackle the end. The end dodges around him and sprints into the clear. The quarterback stops pretending he doesn't have the ball and throws it to the end. Then it does get physical.

The beauty of the play action pass is that it drives the defense crazy. A typical play action pass is diagrammed in Figure 28.

It must be obvious by now that there are an almost infinite number of possible variations to these basic pass routes and designs. Design one for yourself. All you need are a supply of circles, boxes, dotted lines, and arrows.

3

Offensive Line Play

The television cameras zoom in on the quarterback dropping back twelve yards, looking one way to confuse the defense and then throwing the ball a full thirty-five yards into the waiting arms of the receiver. The play-by-play announcer talks about the kind of pattern run by the 9.3 sprinter with the golden hands who can outjump any defender on the field. Every once in a great while, the color man, an ex-professional football player, mentions that the left side of the line "blew out" the defensive line.

They call the game between the two lines "the battle in the trenches" or "fighting in the pit." These are apt metaphors. It's hand-to-hand combat, and all the hero's brilliance and all the coach's genius is meaningless if the war isn't won in the trenches.

The offensive line opens up the holes through which the backs run. The offensive line protects the quarterback when he throws. The offensive line gives way on draws. The offensive line forms the screen. The offensive line provides the interference that makes a power sweep possible. Its play makes mediocre teams look good and good teams look great. The opposite is also true.

The offensive line consists of a center, two guards, two tackles, and those hybrid linemen/backs, the ends. The ones in the middle are referred to as the interior linemen. What an interior lineman has to do is block, block, block. A block is like a no-hands tackle, which is one of the things that makes it hard to play the line. Humans rely so much on their hands that it almost goes against nature not to use them. But the rule is, use your shoulder, use your body, but curl one pinky around any part of your opponent's anatomy or uniform and you get a penalty, if the official sees you. That no-hands rule is probably the single most active cause of dyspeptic ulcers among practicing offensive linesmen in professional football.

Let's have a look at blocking. The soldiers in the trenches, the interior linemen, start operations from the *three-point stance*. That stance is shown in Figure 29. It's called a three-point stance because the body is supported at three points; the feet and one hand. This automatically places the body into a deep crouch. One foot is behind the other in an about-to-charge position. For right-handed people, the right hand is on the ground and the right foot the rearmost. The left arm rests across the left thigh, prepared to be a battering ram. The body placements are reversed for the left-handed (this is known as a sinister development, since the word sinister originally meant on the left side, or un-lucky). The body weight rests on the balls of the feet. The hand on the ground is for balance only. The head is supposed to be up so he can watch the defense. Having assumed this position to test it out, we find it works fine except for the shooting pains in the thighs after several minutes and the recurring headaches.

Once he has assumed that stance, the interior linemen has to freeze until the ball is snapped. His body is square to the

figure 29
Three-point stance

defense and his eyes are on the man in front of him. What he really sees, nobody knows. We have often wondered what goes through the mind of an offensive lineman just before he is going to batter and be battered. He typically weighs in the neighborhood of 270 to 285 pounds, and stands a good six feet five inches. His opponent is only slightly larger. These are young elephants. In the moments before scrimmage, do their minds wander off into fields of blooming daisies? Do butterflies flutter by in their mind's eye? Unknown. What is known is that the coach wants his linemen concentrating on the job ahead — mayhem and confrontation and protect your man but don't use your hands (if you think an official is watching).

Now there he is, on the line waiting for the signal that tells him the ball is snapped. He springs forward right on the count. He knows that the play is designed to run to the left, then through the space to his right. He plunges forward hard and fast, jamming his shoulder and neck into the torso of the

figure 30
Shoulder block

---

opposing player and driving him to the side away from the play. The attempt here is to push the defender into a more upright position; "stand him up" is the jargon in the trade. Once he is upright and the offensive man has his momentum going, it is very hard for the defender to keep from being driven back. The offensive tackle or guard is leaning all of his weight forward and his legs are churning like pistons gone mad. That's one version of the *shoulder block* (Figure 30).

Then there is a little ballet movement known as the *cross-body block*. This block is very often used in what are known as open field situations, or out of the tangle and wrestling match that the line quickly becomes. It usually happens when the offensive player is running interference for a running back. He has to knock down the defender to provide some running room for the ball carrier. Figure 31

figure 31
Cross-body block

---

shows how that happens. The only things missing from the illustration are the smacking sounds produced by the two rushing bodies coming to a sudden stop and the grunt of sudden involuntary exhalation caused by the brief but violent encounter.

Here is a typical cross-body block situation. A short hook-out pattern has been run by one of the backs. It looks like a big gainer, but the free safety is zeroed in and coming fast. That individual weighs something over an eighth of a ton and has had fifteen or twenty yards to build up speed. What happens now is an open field cross-body block. When the safety is less than one body distance away, the blocker throws himself across the safety's upper legs, taking the brunt of the impact against his own arm, shoulder, ribs, and

---

internal organs. Football is more than occasionally a contact sport.

This is a good time to bring up the subject of a *clip*, which is not considered cricket. A clip will bring a fifteen-yard penalty as a personal foul, and occurs when the cross-body (or any other type of block) takes place from behind. A block is from the front or the side. A clip is from behind. Where the side becomes the behind is a judgment call, made by the officials. On some of the close ones, nobody, including the official, knows how the judgment is made. More on that in the chapter on penalties.

Another type of block, the *head-up block*, is usually used when the quarterback is preparing to pass. The quarterback takes the snap and drops back into a "pocket" formed by the offensive linemen. There are two ways a quarterback makes his drop, the backpedal, Figure 32, or sideways step, Figure 33. When he backpedals, he runs backward a given number

figure 32
Quarterback's backpedal

figure 33 **Quarterback's sideways step figure**

of yards, spots his intended receiver, swivels to one side, steps up into the pocket, and heaves the oval ball. In the sideways step he takes the ball and runs sideways to his favorite spot and prays that his linemen are going to successfully fight off the opposition.

figure 34
Head-up block

Now for the head-up block, Figure 34. The offenders (linemen and a back or two) get into their positions around the very vulnerable passer, and go into a semi-crouch. The object is to keep the body weight low for a good center of gravity. The defender comes rushing at the quarterback. The offender moves into him to get some momentum, and, bringing his arms across his chest, bangs into him to drive him back. Remember that the offender can't push with his hands or do any grabbing. The defense has no such inhibitions. He can use anything but his head. That is called "spearing" and was a source of many injuries before it was outlawed. The pass offender learns, often the hard way, not to retreat or try to go for the rusher's ankles. If he retreats, someone will sweep him aside, and if he tries for the ankles some kangaroolike defender will jump right over him to get at the quarterback.

On kicking situations, the admonition to not retreat is a must. The poor kicker needs time, as does the passer, to get off the kick. He can't run away or hide.

4

Doing It for Kicks

When the game of American football developed out of British rugby, there was no such thing as the forward pass. You could run the ball or you could kick it to one of your teammates. Now, it is doubtful if anybody living remembers seeing a dropkick to a wide receiver. What is left of the kicking game consists of point-after-touchdowns, conversions, punts, field goals, and kickoffs.

Kickers are a strange breed. When you look at the specialized physical and mental attributes of, say, quarterbacks, you can see many commonalities. Most quarterbacks are good all-around athletes, with good hand-eye coordination, tall and rangy builds, strong arms, quick feet, and a talent for leadership. They tend to be intelligent, decisive, confident, courageous, even-tempered, articulate, and all-purpose candidates for leadership in industry. Defensive linemen are all very big, have facial hair they they cut and sell for steel wool pads to major restaurant chains, mean dispositions, enjoy body contact (that is, they love to hit and be hit), and fire themselves up before the game by banging their heads against each other and various brick walls.

Kickers, on the other hand, have only one thing in common. They kick footballs. They come in all sizes and shapes, exhibit a great deal of athletic ability or absolutely none, kick the ball with special shoes or no shoes at all, are overweight, underweight, extremely articulate, or don't speak English any better than the mad monk, Rasputin. Tom Dempsey (now retired) had no toes on his kicking foot. He wore a special shoe. A dynamite kicker. Famous quarterback, George Blanda, extended his playing days into his early fifties by becoming a kicker and scoring the most points in football. As of this writing, Blanda still holds that record. He was "retired" against his will and could probably go back out there and score a few more points if anyone let him.

What is important about kickers is that nobody cares what a kicker looks like, sounds like, thinks like, or for that matter, smells like. What a kicker has to do is stand in there with the whole defensive team rushing in to smother him and the ball before it gets high in the air. He has nowhere to go. He must depend on his blockers to keep out the defense. On top of that, every time he goes out on the field to do his thing, it's an emergency situation (except for kickoffs). The pressures are immediate, sharp, but fleeting. He can win or lose the whole shooting match with one stroke of his magic foot. No wonder they are very individual.

The ball game starts off with the kickoff. There are two ways to kick a ball, *straight-on* (Figure 35) or *soccer-style* (Figure 36). In the straight-on kick, as its name implies, the kicker comes to the ball from directly behind it and hits it with his toe. Soccer-style kickers approach the ball diagonally, usually about 45 degrees, and hit the ball with their instep. The ball is usually put on a kicking tee for the kickoff. There are some kickers who prefer to make a hole in the ground and prop it up that way. It's hard to imagine making a

figure 35
Straight-on placekick

figure 36
Soccer-style placekick

hole in artificial turf without a pneumatic drill and diamond bit. Each kicker has his own preference for the number of steps he has to make in order to get tothe ball—about seven yards is average.

The object of the kickoff is to (1) get the ball high in the air, turning end-over-end, (2) get the ball far downfield, (3) keep the ball inbounds, (4) give the kicking special team plenty of time to get downfield in time to tackle the catcher.

Kickoffs start each half of the game and are used after a touchdown or field goal to turn the ball over to the opposing team. One variation of the kickoff is the attempt *not* to turn the ball over to the opposing team. This is called the *onside kick*. It is used when a team is losing near the end of the game and has just scored some points. They want another chance at running the football on offense. All of their good ball handlers situate themselves on the line, and the kicker "squibs" the ball, that is, kicks it so it bounces along the ground. It has to go at least ten yards and then it's anybody's ball.

On an ordinary start-of-the-game-type kickoff, the special team lines up behind the line of scrimmage. (The ball sits on its tee on the line of scrimmage). At his signal, the kicker starts toward the ball. The rule says that nobody is supposed to cross the line until the ball has been kicked. Then it's helter-skelter toward the poor unfortunate who stands way back watching the wildly gyrating ovoid come down out of the blue. He has to concentrate on catching the ball and pay no attention to the thundering herd stampeding toward him.

If the ball is not caught, the kicking team can ground it by touching the ball. Play starts there. If the ball is caught, the kicking team tries to ground the receiver. They are usually rougher on the receiver than they are on the ball. Grounding the ball consists of touching it, but when they knock the receiver down, they get very literal and try to grind him into the ground. If the ball is touched by any member of the receiving team and not kept in possession, the ball is fair game. Whichever side gets it, keeps it. Kick returners have learned to let the ball land untouched if the prospects of catching it don't look good.

The catcher has one more option; he can call for a "fair catch." He signals the whole world by raising one arm high in the air. That means, "I am going to catch the ball and not run with it after I get my paws on it. If anybody messes with me, I'll tell the officials and they will chide you on your deportment and give my team some yardage." After he signals for a fair catch, he'd better make one, since it looks terrible to be not interfered with and not catch the ball. Bobbling it can be more than embarrassing; it could lead to a turnover.

Punts are a very important part of the game. A team punts when it hasn't made a first down (you remember the first down, don't you?). It is a way of giving the ball to the other side in as disadvantageous a position as possible. The perfect punt goes out of bounds on the 1-inch line with an official there to call it.

The person who kicks punts may or may not be the same person who does the kickoff or PAT work. In a punt, the punter is fair game for the defense providing they get to him before the ball is in the air. If they get to him after the ball has been kicked, there is a penalty for "roughing the kicker." This results in a first down for the kicking team and, instead of turning the ball over to the opposition, they get a reprieve on offense. As a result, there is a rumor that there are acting classes for punters to teach them how to pretend to be hit and fall down in pain.

The ball is also fair game and punt blocking is practiced as a defensive tactic. What usually happens is the punt blocker misses the ball and blocks the kicker. See the preceding paragraph on roughing the kicker.

Figure 37 shows a punt. The punter takes a position

figure 37
Punt

---

fifteen yards behind the center. The backfield forms a protective cadre in front of him. The center snaps the ball back between his knees in an arc. The punter catches it, takes two, three, or four steps, drops the ball and kicks it before it touches the ground.

The point-after-touchdown kick (PAT) is worth one point and has often meant the difference between winning and losing. It is like the punt in that the ball is snapped from the center. But in this case a holder catches the ball, sticks its nose in the ground, and holds it in place with one or two fingers. The ball must be exactly placed and angled so the kicker can aim true and high. True is important as far as aim is concerned. High is important because the defending team is running hard to block the kick.

A field goal is just like the PAT except that it usually takes place from farther away. Both the PAT and the field goal are called placekicks because the holder has to place the ball and hold it. The field goal is worth three points and is an important offensive weapon. When a team can't get the ball into the end zone for a touchdown, they try to get close enough for a field goal. The optimum distance is from about thirty-five yards out, or from about the 25-yard line, taking into account that the goalpost is at the back of the end zone ten yards behind the goal line. Kicks of over fifty yards have been made but they are the exception rather than the rule.

KICK RECEIVING

Receiving a kick is the same whether it's a kickoff or a punt. The receiving team forms two protective lines across the field. The receiver(s) stations himself where he thinks the ball is going to come down and waits for it to happen. If he catches the ball, the receiving team tries to form a protective wedge of blockers in front of him. If he has any smarts, he tries to get behind this wedge, or at least pick up a blocker or two. He then heads as fast as he can toward the enemy territory. What the coach wants is good field position to start the offense. What the receiver wants is to run untouched for a touchdown, or, failing that, a good gain, or not to get hurt too much. This person has to have a very optimistic bent of mind, since the odds are against him.

5

Thou Shalt Not Give Up Yardage

They say that for every offense there is a defense. That may or may not be true. What is true is that for every offensive formation there is a defensive alignment. The object of an offensive formation is to be in the best arrangement for a particular play. The object of a defensive alignment is to stop every play dead and, if possible, throw the opposition for a loss.

A good defensive alignment is prepared to stop either the run or pass. Obviously, if the defense is certain the upcoming play is a run, there's not much point in playing pass defense. The opposite is also true, which is why a team with a large score advantage late in the game has an easy time of it on defense. In most cases, the offense has to throw the ball if there is to be any chance of getting back into contention. The defense can then gear up for its pass defense.

Defensive alignments are usually known by a number. These indicate the proportion of the team assigned to various locations. The total always equals 11. By some coinci-

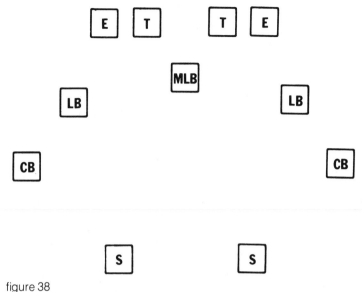

figure 38
The 4-3-2-2- defense

---

dence, that's how many men are on a team. As an illustration, take that old veteran of Sunday wars, the old $4-3-2-2$ *defense.* Notice the total—11. The 4—3—2—2 defense is shown in Figure 38, and consists of end-tackle-tackle-end as the front four linemen. This is backed up by left linebacker-middle linebacker-right linebacker. Behind and to the outside of the linebackers, we find the left and right cornerbacks. Behind them and to the inside are stationed the two safeties. Once you understand the scheme, $4-3-2-2$ is a very handy shorthand. An even shorter shorthand abbreviates the alignment to its bare essentials, $4-3$. The cornerbacks and safeties are implied.

This alignment is all set for either a pass or a run. There are two safeties to grab anybody who makes it past the line. Two cornerbacks are ready to fly out with the potential receivers, and three linebackers are prepared to fill the holes or go to the outside. From this formation a "blitz" is

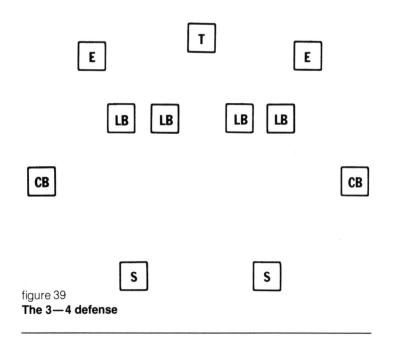

figure 39
The 3—4 defense

---

also a possibility. A blitz is when the linebackers go for the passer (see page 83).

Another formation you are likely to see is the 3–4 shown in Figure 39. The 3–4 puts three men on the line with four linebackers. The linebackers can play up close to the line for a blitz or a run, or can drop back to counter a sweep or a pass. It is a very common alignment in these days of large, quick men.

There are a couple of special situation defenses. One of them is the *prevent defense*, shown in Figure 40. This one is used near the end of the game when the team on defense is ahead, and time is running out, and the other guys have to score to win. The prevent defense permits short gains, even first downs, but prevents a touchdown. It is essentially a 4–3 or a 3–4 with the defensive secondary, the linebackers, cornerbacks, and safeties dropping back to protect from the long gainer.

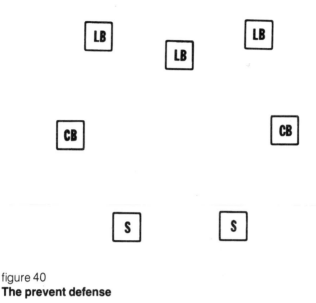

figure 40
The prevent defense

A *goal line defense* is when the opposition has the team squeezed up against the goal line. That alignment is shown in Figure 41. In the goal line defense, everybody is right up close to the line to plug up any holes. The safeties play a little back to protect against the pass.

The tactic on defense consists of an attempt to break up the play by assigning certain positions to certain tasks. Everybody has his man or his zone to take on. The stances taken by each position are part of the type of assignment given to that position. Linemen operate from the three-point stance. They are prepared to shoot out forward or to the side with a maximum of power and drive. The middle linebackers typically stand square to the line in a slight hunched position, ready to charge forward or backpedal as determined by the development of the play. The outside linebackers usually crouch slightly, with one foot forward of the other, prepared to charge toward the ballcarrier, the

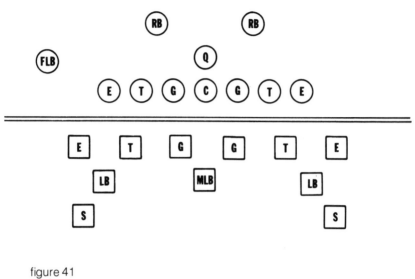

figure 41
The goal line defense

quarterback, or shift to protect their zones (if that is the type of pass defense used).

Everybody on defense reads the *keys*. A key is a clue to what is about to happen. It takes experience and knowledge to read a key. The good defensive player knows what they mean.

For example, if an offensive lineman charges more than a yard or two forward, the experienced linebacker knows a run is coming up. How, you ask? "Because," he will answer, "if the play is to be a pass, he can't go that far forward without being penalized as an ineligible receiver downfield."

Alternatively, if the offensive lineman drops back and throws a pass protection block, the defense can count on a pass, so it's "drop into the pass defense position."

To make sure that each and every key is read and understood, each defensive team member is assigned to watch at least two opponents throughout the game. As the play starts to break, he looks for tips as to the direction of the play and the type of play being run. If one of his assigned opponents breaks to one side it may tell the watcher the direction of the play. The way the other one moves may tip off the type of play. The defensive linemen have a little tactic they call the *grab and shake.* Since they can use their hands and the offense cannot, they take advantage of that rule. In grab and shake, at the snap of the ball, they grab the offensive lineman by the shoulder, give him a push to one side, and try to charge past him on the other side. This operation is performed quickly and with a minimum of gentleness. They shake hard and then push even more roughly. If done correctly, the lineman receiving this treatment feels foolish as hell watching his opponent come roaring by him. He is then tempted to either hold or clip, both of which are highly illegal.

Tackling is a much misunderstood term. A tackle can be made from the front, the side, or the rear. Tackles from the front tend to be rare. Usually, if the guy being tackled can see the tackler coming head on, he can elude the tackle. Most tackles are from the side or rear. A tackle, to all intents and purposes, is just knocking somebody to the ground. Grabbing an ankle and making the other player fall down is a tackle. The famous flying tackle of yesteryear is forbidden in the modern game. The flying tackle consisted of a swan dive without a swimming pool or diving board, soaring through the air like an eagle and grabbing the ball carrier with both arms around his thighs or other part of the body.

The most common tackle that gets "slipped" is the arm tackle. This one depends on trying to pull the opponent to the ground by strength of arms alone. The opponent is usually far too strong for this tactic to work. He just keeps on running and the tackler is left with the sometimes unsettling view of the rear of the runner as seen from the ground.

Pass defense provides a lot of excitement during the

figure 42a and b
Head-on tackle

game. There are three basic types of pass defense: *zone defense*, *man-to-man defense*, and a little gem called the *blitz*. Most teams play either a man-to-man, usually with an occasional zone if the situation warrants it, or a zone defense with an occasional man-to-man thrown in just to mess up the works. Everybody uses the blitz at one time or another. Some teams use it a lot more than others do.

The zone is somewhat more vulnerable to the short pass than the man-to-man is, so if the opposition is known as a short yardage passing team, a team whose defense is primarily zone may switch to man-to-man. The opposite is obviously also true. However, some teams are so confident of their man-to-man or zone defense that they always play it.

A zone defense is a way of breaking up the downfield areas into defensive zones and assigning a defensive secondary player to protect against a pass thrown in his zone. When the would-be receiver is in one zone, that zone's defensive back has the responsibility of keeping him from catching a pass. When the receiver goes into the next person's zone, it's the next player's responsibility. This leads inexorably to "seams" where the zones border on each other. In theory there is an overlap. In practice, there are many passers and receivers who make a good living throwing and catching passes into the seams. This is a drawback to the zone defense, yet this type of defense does spread the burden and relieves the pass defenders from the onerous job of staying with some of the super-fast, golden-handed receivers who operate so flashily in the defensive backfield. A typical zone defense is shown in Figure 43.

Man-to-man defense is, as its name implies, the assignment of a defensive back to a given receiver. As a rule, linebackers are assigned to cover backs out of the offensive backfield. Their job is breaking up the short pass. Cornerbacks go with the wide receiver with the possible assistance of a safety. Typically, the free safety goes with a cornerback.

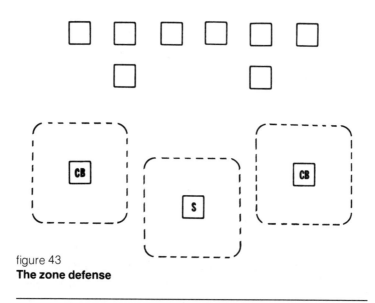

figure 43
The zone defense

The strong safety (called that not because he is any stronger than the weak safety—who may or may not be free—but because he plays on the side where the tight end is stationed) is usually assigned to cover the tight end. On a two-tight-end offense, there is no free safety, and it's catch-as-catch-can. A three-tight-end offense usually means a running play with the tight ends in for more blocking.

In a man-to-man defense, the defender stays with his assigned receiver and tries to keep between him and the goal. Cornerbacks usually stay very close to their man and make most of the interceptions. The pass defenders are considered bona fide pass receivers and have as much right to catch the ball, if they can, as the offensive receiver does.

In every pass defense case, the object is to try to intercept the football, knock the ball away, tackle the receiver or knock him out of bounds as soon as possible after the reception. A pass defender cannot interfere with the receiver in such a way that he can't catch the pass. If he grabs him, tackles him, or even makes contact with him any time after

---

the first five yards beyond the line of scrimmage, before the ball is caught, that's a defensive pass interference. Defensive pass interference is an automatic first down at the place of the infraction.

Conversely, if the defensive type is going after the ball and is interfered with by the offensive receiver, that's offensive pass interference and a penalty is assessed on the offense. For details of penalties, see Chapter Seven.

Then we have the blitz, or red dog, or just plain dog as they used to call it. The diagram of Figure 44 shows a typical blitz. The blitz is used to pressure the passer and even sack him for a loss when the defense knows (or thinks it knows) he is going to pass. In a blitz, linebackers shoot through the

figure 44
The blitz

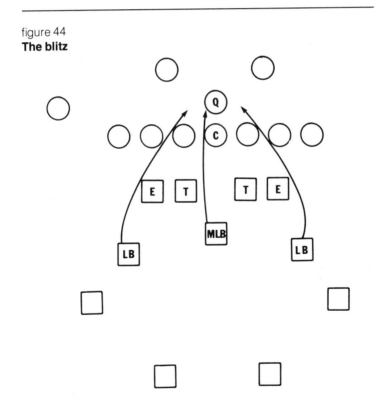

line, or around it if they have to, joined by their linemen, and attempt to grab, knock down, smother, inundate, dismember, and grind into dust the opposition passer before he can pass. That's the key to the blitz. If they do those things before he passes, it's legal. If they do it to him after he passes, that's *roughing the passer*, which brings a nice penalty. Of course, if a rusher's forward motion cannot be contained, and he gets to the quarterback after the ball is thrown, it's acceptable. The newest rule, designed to save the life and limb of quarterbacks, hold that if the passer is in the arms of the defender, the play is over and the defender may not destroy his prey.

The blitz is a gamble. Once a team commits itself to the blitz, the pass coverage is thin and, if the quarterback is quick enough, the pass has a good chance of completion. You pays your money and yer takes yer cherce, as they say in Brooklyn.

6

Strategy

Strategy is the art of applying tactics. As soon as one game is over, preparations are started for the next game. A *game plan* is developed. That game plan is strategy. If you are the head coach of an NFL team, or a sandlot aggregation for that matter, you want a game plan that takes advantage of the opposition team's weaknesses and your team's strengths. Conversely, you want to compensate for your team's weaknesses and not play into the opposition's strength.

In professional ball, all of the opposition's previously played game films are examined to determine both the characteristic game philosophy and pinpoint strengths and weaknesses, offensively and defensively. Individual players are focused upon, their every movement perused and analyzed. Idiosyncratic mannerisms are examined for clues as to what reactions they appear to predict. These are fed into a computer for statistical evaluation. If, for instance, an outside linebacker always fakes into the line (stunts) twice, then tries to slip around the tight end in an attempt to sack the quarterback, that particular mannerism might be something to watch for. If that same linebacker and his cohorts usually rush the passer on the third and long, the plan might be to call a lot of draw plays in that situation. That's strategy.

Another decision can result from looking at the kind of pass defense a team uses. Team A, for example, uses a zone defense 80 percent of the time. Perhaps they do this because the defensive coordinator comes from a team that features such a defense and it is the only one he really knows, or perhaps team A doesn't have a pass defender who can keep up with a fast receiver. Team B uses that situation to its advantage by planning to throw a lot of short passes into the seams between the zones.

Another example of offensive game planning is derived from an examination of the team strength. In this example, the offensive line is especially strong on the left side. The guard and tackle on that side "blow out" the defense on just about every play. The plan therefore would be to run lots of slants and sweeps to the left side.

The defensive game plan develops in a similar manner. If a weakness is noted on the opposition's offense, it is taken advantage of. For instance, the fullback has a tendency to block straight ahead and to his left, but cannot move to his right quite as fast as a result of an old injury. The defensive tactic would be to blitz to his right when rushing the passer. The strategy would be to blitz often to that side.

Pass defense takes advantage of the defender's strengths. Say he is very fast and has "good hands." The strategy might be to go for a lot of interceptions. This takes the chance of leaving the field open behind the receiver if the defender tries for an interception and fails; on the other hand, if it succeeds often enough, it might convince the offense to shy away from long passes into that particular defender's area.

Once a game plan has been developed by the coaches and given the seal of acceptance by the head coach, the plan is explained to the players. All players are given instructions on the game plan, but the people most responsible for carrying it out are given the most attention. These people are the quarterbacks and the team captains, offensive and defensive. The quarterback on many teams has to call the play on the line. On other teams, the offensive plays are called by the coaches. Some teams use signals to convey play calling if the coaches decide the plays. Other teams shuttle in players with the call from the bench. Defensive calls are usually made on the field. Sometimes a coach or spotter in the stands notices something that might result in a recommendation to the call player. These spotters are in constant communication by field telephone with the bench. They have a view not available from field level and can strongly affect the game plan. There is usually an overall game plan with preset modifications built in for the second half, but with enough flexibility to take advantage of information learned during the game.

One of the greatest joys of watching a game is to figure out the game plan and predict the call. If you are right, you feel great. If you are wrong, well, after all, *they're* the pros. Enjoy!

7

Zebras — The Officials

There is a small striped horse that lives on the African plains that is constantly being chased by lions, cheetahs, panthers, leopards, and zoo keepers. Another kind of zebra, also striped, spends some time on the football field every Sunday and Monday night, with an occasional Thursday night and Saturday afternoon thrown in. This zebra gets revenge for his African namesake. He harasses Eagles, Lions, Falcons, Rams, Raiders, and even Giants. These zebras, the officials, so-called because of their striped shirts, share one other equine characteristic. Like horses, you can lead them to water, but you can't make them drink. When an official makes his call, it is irreversible. An official never changes his mind. Neither the entreaties of coaches, players, one hundred thousand fans, nor the instant television replay has any effect. He calls what he sees and what he has called is the way it is—period, end of sentence.

Maybe that's the way it ought to be. After all, he is right there on the field, right next to whatever happened. And maybe the perfection of electronic recordings has no place in football, which is a game between humans, expressing human emotions and human failings. Maybe there is already too much of the mechanical in our lives, game lives or real. Still, sometimes it would be nice if on some of the close calls a referee could look at four different views of the incident in question as recorded on videotape, and say, "Sorry, world, we were in error. The tape shows that the ball receiver caught the pass with both feet inbound and the touchdown counts. Please forgive us."

In a professional football game there are seven officials who are responsible for making the calls and keeping order on the field. They are the final arbiters of everything that goes on on the field.

The *referee* is the boss. He supervises the conduct of the game and his word is, you guessed it, LAW. He gives all the signals, describes the infraction to the watching national public, and is final judge in any argument or interpretation. He also spots the ball, a responsibility almost awesome in its implications. How many first downs have been tipped one way or the other by the position the ball has been spotted in? What about some of those touchdowns (or missed ones) where a sixty-fourth of an inch makes the difference? The referee positions himself ten to twelve yards deep in the offensive backfield and turns his eagle eye on the quarterback.

The *umpire* is responsible for watching that the players conduct themselves like perfect gentlemen on the field. He starts the play about five yards downfield. One of the things he looks for are illegal chucks. Once the lines have charged each other, he hangs around the open field with one hand on a yellow handkerchief stuck in his back pocket. All officials have them. They are not for nose blowing or brow mopping. They are the flags, dropped or thrown in the event of a detected rule infraction. Some umpires are of the fast-draw variety and take their inspiration from Wyatt Earp. Others are "late droppers." On the whole, they strike a happy medium. The umpire has jurisdiction over equipment.

The *head linesman* is responsible for observing the neutral zone and calling those annoying false starts and offside penalties. He is one of the officials on the lookout for pass interference as well as blocking infractions. He also makes sure that the "chain gang" are on their toes. His responsibilities include keeping track of the down and yards-to-go situations.

The *line judge* situates himself astraddle the line of scrimmage opposite the linesman. He does some of the same things the linesman does, but he is also charged with keeping time of the game as a backup for the game clock. He watches the receiver as he comes downfield for the first seven yards, then goes into the backfield to make sure that a forward pass actually goes forward. He also checks whether the passer is behind the line of scrimmage when he lets go of the ball. He counts the time-outs, is in charge of the coin toss, and monitors the score. He rules on whether or not a punt crosses the line of scrimmage and generally rules on the blocking game.

The *back judge* stations himself seventeen yards downfield, watches the receiver, and observes that the offensive backs throw legal blocks. He watches the deep receivers to make sure they catch the ball with both feet inbounds.

The *side judge* has the good judgment to be on the same side of the field as the linesman, but about seventeen yards downfield. That puts him right across from the back judge, and they share a lot of the same responsibilities, including watching for illegal blocks, loose balls, and keeping an eye on the sidelines on their sides of the field.

The *field judge* is stationed twenty-five yards downfield, usually on the same side as the tight end. Among his other tasks are monitoring the thirty-second clock and calling the infraction if it is exceeded.

The rule book defines sixty-seven infractions with a pre-scribed penalty for each. Some of them are obvious and readily understood, some subtle and require a deep knowledge of the game. Some of them require use of a corporate law firm for interpretation. Then there are some which defy the best minds in jurisprudence, science, and theology. A list of the most common infractions and their penalties is given below.

Infraction	Definition	Penalty
Offside	A player with any part of his body over the line of scrimmage or free kick line *when the ball is snapped.*	5 yards
Encroachment	A player is caught in the neutral zone at the time of the snap, or makes con-tact with the opposi-tion *before the ball is snapped.*	5 yards
Delay of game	The thirty-second clock runs out before the play gets off.	5 yards

Infraction	Definition	Penalty
	Other situations are up to the official's judgment.	
Running into the kicker	That's running into him before the ball is kicked. Not called if an offensive player knocks the miscreant into the kicker.	Automatic first down and 5 yards
Roughing the kicker	See above, with more energy and after he kicked the ball. A judgment call.	Automatic first down and 15 yards
Roughing the passer	Another judgment call. Occurs after the passer has released the ball.	Automatic first down and 15 yards
Face mask	Two versions of this infraction, and definitely a judgment call. Type 1: grasping the face mask. If by the defense. . . If by the offense . . . Type 2: twisting, turning,	Automatic first down 5 yards

Infraction	Definition	Penalty
	or pulling an opponent by the face mask. If by the defense . . .	Automatic first down and 15 yards
Clipping	Throwing the body across the back of an opponent's legs, or hitting him from behind, unless the opponent is a runner.	15 yards
Defensive holding	Illegal use of the hands. This is such a complicated call that we must refer you to the official Digest of Rules, for a description of this infraction.	Automatic first down and 15 yards
Offensive holding	Illegal use of the hands. For further information, look this up in the Digest of Rules.	10 yards
Intentional grounding	When the passer throws the ball away to avoid a loss of yardage	10 yards and loss of down

Infraction	Definition	Penalty
	when he is about to be sacked. The infraction must be very apparent. If there is the slightest possibility that there is a would-be receiver in the vicinity of the ball, the call is an incomplete pass.	
Interference with a fair catch	When a fair catch is signaled on a kicking play, the receiver may not be touched by an opposition player.	15 yards from the point of infraction
Unsportsman-like conduct	Strictly a judgment call. The officials judge kind of conduct sportsmen do not indulge in.	15 yards

The list goes on.

Each infraction has a corresponding signal, a gyration by the referee. He waves his arms, pats the top of his head, performs a karate chop aimed at this own knee. These are shown in the following illustrations. The beauty of these signals is that you don't really have to hear what the misconduct is. The signal tells the whole story. In fact, it is only since small radio transmitters were perfected that the referee announced his decision to the listening public. Now, he is practically an entertainer on national TV. Possibly he takes elocution and movement lessons. All he needs now is a good joke writer.

First down

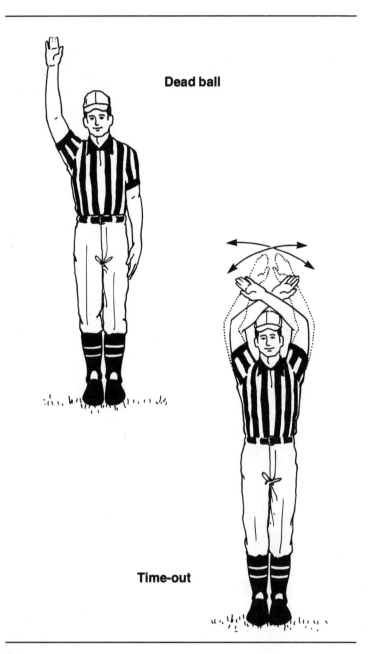

Dead ball

Time-out

**No time-out
start clock**

**Delay of game
excess time-out**

**Illegal formation
or procedure**

**Running into or
roughing the kicker
(personal foul)**

**Clipping
(personal foul)**

**Illegal receiver or
member of the kicking team
downfield**

**Interference with a
forward pass or
fair catch
Illegal**

Invalid fair catch

Ball illegally kicked, touched, or batted

Illegal conduct

Illegal motion at the snap

Illegally touching a forward pass or scrimmage kick

Loss of down

Holding

Crawling, pushing, or helping the ballcarrier

Running into or roughing the passer (personal foul)

Illegal crackback

Illegal forward pass

**Illegal cut or
blocking below the waist**

**Intentional grounding
of a pass**

Invalid fair catch signal

Pass juggled inbounds but caught out of bounds

Illegal use of
the hands

Holding

Tripping

**Grabbing the face mask
(personal foul)**

Penalty refused/ incomplete pass/ play over/missed goal

Player ejected

Touchdown/field goal/ PAT

Safety

8

The Organization

Pro football is more than a game, it is a business. Big business. It makes its owners very wealthy just from television revenues alone. Weak teams or strong, loser or winner, every team in the NFL gets an equal share of league revenues from the sale of broadcast rights to the major networks. Add to this the ticket sale revenues, a percentage in many cases of the concession revenues, parking, and souvenirs; it all adds up to a tidy sun.

Who owns the NFL teams? It varies. Some teams are privately owned by an individual or his family, some are partnerships. One team is owned in part by a community, Green Bay, Wisconsin. When one of the owners of the Packers wanted to move the team franchise to a different city, the citizens of that town were offered an opportunity to buy out his shares to keep the team. They did and now the Green Bay Packers are, in the best sense of the word, community owned. The Chicago Bears, on the other hand, are still owned by "Papa Bear" George Halas, who helped form the league back in the twenties. There's Pat Rooney, who "fathered" the Pittsburgh Steelers. Whatever the arrangement, and just about every imaginable one is represented in the NFL, there must be romance in owning a football team because the owners appear to love the game. They love the excitement, the color, the ambience, the celebrity, and above all the power and joy that comes with winning.

What makes up a football team besides the players? The organization, which sounds a little like the Cosa Nostra, but it isn't. The organization includes the coaches, the trainers, the doctors, the personnel people (including scouts), the groundskeepers, the public relations flacks, the cheerleaders, the band, the front office clerks. Add all the people who sell the hot dogs and beer, the team pennants and T-shirts, the plastic helmets and the numbered jersey in sizes 3 to 12 for boys and girls both, the parking attendants and the part-time program vendor working his way through college, and you have some idea of the vastness of the organization.

Of course, the whole thing rests like an inverted pyramid on the broad shoulders of the forty-five athletes who play the game. Players last on the average from three to five years; coaches usually last a lot longer if they win, but are at the mercy of the whims of the ownership. The owners go on forever, or so it seems.

The coaches run the team, figuratively and literally. They run the practices and make the players run: run laps, run the forty-yard dash, run from scrimmage and to scrimmage. The coaches run off their charges' fat, accumulated over the lazy off-season. The coaches run on the muscle necessary to "out physical" the opposition. The coaches also run their mouths, yelling, explaining, teaching, cajoling, and occasionally threatening the players.

At the top of the coaching heap is the *head coach*. He's the boss, except for the big boss, the owner. Under the head coach are the specialty coaches like the *offensive coordinator*, the *defensive coordinator*, the *line coach*, the *backfield coach*, the *kicking coach*, the *catching coach*, the *passing coach*, the offensive and defensive *special team coaches* and probably one or two more. All these coaches fine tune the team in their particular specialty.

The responsibility of the offensive and defensive coordinators is to develop strategy. They are very important in developing a game plan. Much of the "look" a team shows, which is credited to the head coach, is actually generated by these two coordinators and their staff. However, in the final analysis, it is the head coach whose character sets the tone for the team. And often enough, he takes his cue from the owner's personality.

As you would expect, head coaches have strong personalities. There are wide variations in how these personalities express themselves. Stoic Tom Landry, the only head coach the Dallas Cowboys have ever had, was the first coach in football to employ the modern electronic computer as a team building and coaching aid.

The ex-coach of the Oakland Raiders, Big John Madden, engaged in sideline antics that were almost as fun to watch as the on-field brouhaha. He was very fine coach with one of the great records in football, but he got so involved he had to quit to save himself from galloping ulcers and heart failure.

Bum Phillips thrusts out his massive jaw, squirts tobacco juice a full twenty yards, leans back on his high-heeled cowboy boots, shoves back his stetson, waves his arms like a berserk windmill, and curses in pure southwestern when something goes wrong. Another fine coach.

What they all have in common is the overwhelming need to win and the leadership talent to get the athletes to do it for them. These are the men who have final say on game strategy, team image, style, and attitude.

Trainers spend a lot of time taping forearms and wrists.

They stick elbows and knees into whirlpool baths, give out vitamins and other pills, help players condition themselves, prescribe weight and strength exercises, and generally look after the health and well-being of the team. When a player is injured on the field and someone comes running out to examine the fallen warrior, that's the trainer. They often work with the equipment men and have helped design some braces and aids to protect injured areas that permit a player to go back on the field.

The personnel people are the unsung heroes. They are also very important in the organization. The personnel they deal with are not the secretaries and accounting clerks, but player personnel. They scout the colleges and universities on the lookout for the one-in-a-million phenomenon, the super player that nobody else knows about. The one they can "steal" as a ninth-round draft choice. Actually, that's a fantasy. Every team has computer data on every prospect. The scouts know more about a college player than he knows about himself. They know how he runs, what his sexual proclivities are, his attitude, his physical strength, and his mental stability, as well as his body measurements and school athletic records. The college drafts that make tomorrow's teams are decided largely by player personnel.

Personnel staff also help make decisions about who gets put on waivers, who gets back on the team, and who gets cut loose. The head coach and general manager make the final decisions, but the manager of player personnel has his say. Building a team requires an outstanding player personnel department.

Football is in the entertainment business, and therefore takes on some of the attributes more usually associated with Hollywood and the Ringling Bros., Barnum and Bailey Circus—hype, more politely known as public relations. PR covers a multitude of sins: press relations, "leaks" to favored sports columnists or reporters, press releases on team policy, anything to keep the public aware of the team's existance. PR men are also dedicated to protecting the good name by denying rumors, sanitizing scandals, and presenting the team, its owners, and players in the best possible light.

PR men carefully groom the superstars for their meetings with the press. They provide the booze that lubricates the sportswriters and mellows their cynicism. Sportswriters tend to be frustrated athletes, too small, too uncoordinated, too slow to play the game competitively. So they write about it. It is a vicarious experience and does put them into the exclusive world of professional sports. In other words, they're romantics and an easy sell. Half of what you read in the sports pages or hear in the features on the sports broadcasts originates on the PR man's desk. The other half he denies anyway.

Cheerleaders look like they were left over from the June Taylor Dancers, who made it big on the old Jackie Gleason Show. Pretty girls dressed in scanty costumes of team colors kick and shake their way through the game on the sidelines. They dance to the team band music, jiggle and juggle their pompons, and excite the crowd to ecstasies of pulchritudinous pandemonium. These are pretty ladies. All volunteers, they get no pay, spend a lot of time practicing their jiggling and dance steps, and pose for a lot of male chauvinistic TV cameramen.

Every year, there are replacements for women who go on to bigger and better things, develop middle-aged spread, or are just plain "jiggled out." When the call goes out, the volunteers apply in droves. The selection process is rigorous by any definition. The standards are definite and more than a little arbitrary. Of course, the candidates must be able to kick and wiggle in unison. Hollywood beauty standards prevail. There is usually a healthy contingent of blondes, bottled, tinted or God-given. The whole thing is as American as apple pie, the county fair, and hard contact football.

The groundskeepers keep the grounds. If the turf is mowable, they mow it; if it is sewable, they sew it. They also cover the field when it rains, and do all the crummy jobs no one else wants to do. But they can be important to the outcome of the game, since they can prepare the field to provide a home field advantage. It's a very subtle business, but, for example, if the home team is used to natural grass and the visitors aren't, the groundskeepers leave the turf longer than they ordinarily would, reasoning that the visitors will be used to a fast surface and the home team to a slower one. Tricky, eh?

Though the concession people may consider it "their" team, especially when the team is winning, there exists a problem between the concessionaires and the team ownership in several cities. There is a lot of money in the concessions, and the team ownership would like a part of it. In many cities the concession licenses belong to the stadium, and the stadium belongs to the city or to a separate corporation, not to the team owners. This has led to acrimonious discussions at times with the team owners saying, "Give me a bigger share, or I'll pack my bags, team and all and I'll move to another city that will love me more."

This illustrates the dilemma created by football as a business. Businesses make money, as much as possible within the legal constraints that exist. But football generates love and loyalty and fanatic devotion on the part of some fans. How is that loyalty to be repaid? What does the team ownership owe to the devoted followers of the team as a result? We don't have the answer, and there certainly isn't one single simple answer, but the questions need thought and consideration by all those involved.

CHOOSING UP SIDES

A football team consists of eleven men, at least on the playing field. But how many men can there be on a football team? Well, that depends partly on what time of the year it is, and on whom you consider a member of the team.

A team can open its training camp during the summer with an unlimited number of players, but very shortly that number gets cut, limited, and sorted into groups.

There is an *active list* and a *reserve list,* which is further divided into the *injured reserve,* the *retired reserve* and the *other reserve.*

On the active list are those players under contract, including those playing out their option, who are eligible to play in the pre-season, regular season, and the post-season games. By the middle of August, a team must have cut its active list to sixty players, and by the end of August the number has to be down to fifty players. Thus the pre-season games are a testing, culling process to determine who will stay with a team and who will be released. By the first part of September, the beginning of the regular season, the active list is limited to forty-five players. These numbers can vary slightly from year to year, but these are the exact numbers used since 1978 and are generally accurate.

The reserve list consists of those players who, because of injuries, retirement, military service, or other circumstances are not immediately available to play for a team, even though they are still under contract to that team.

A player placed on the injured reserve who is physically unable to play for a period of four weeks after being put on the list can be reinstated, as active, if the team complies with the *waiver recall* procedures (see below). In addition, the team is allowed to designate three of its players for *free recall* if they were placed on the injured reserve after the final cut at the begining of the regular season. Sounds complicated, but it means if a valuable player is injured during the season, they can get him back playing if he gets better. This is limited to three players; the others may have to stay out the whole season.

Now, what is the waiver system? This is a procedure set up by the NFL in which a player's contract or the NFL rights to that player are made available to other teams. During the claiming period, usually a ten-day period during the off-season, the other teams file a claim to the player or give up (waive) the opportunity to file. Claiming clubs are assigned players on a priority basis rooted in the inverse of their won/lost record. In other words, the poorer a team played the previous year, the better chance they have to obtain a player through the waiver procedure. Sometime between July and December there is an additional twenty-four-hour period in which the original team is allowed to rescind its action (it withdraws its offer of the player—known as a "recall of a waiver request"). In the same period the claiming team can withdraw its offer for a player (known as a "withdrawal of claim").

Any player who passes through waivers unclaimed and not recalled by his own team becomes a *free agent*. He can go to any team and sell his own services—if he's a super salesman or has a good agent he may make a great deal. In addition, because of the growing emphasis on players' rights, any player who has earned four years' pension credits and is about to be assigned to a new team can refuse the assignment and become a free agent.

The waiver system is a part of the trading of players that goes on between the teams of the NFL. Trading between the NFC and AFC is unrestricted after the post-season and through about the middle of October. Players are traded for money, other players, draft choices, or any or all of these in combination.

Draft-round positions are assigned in the same inverse

ratio to the previous year's won/lost standings as assignment of players acquired by waiver. A team with a good winning record may trade a player for some team's high draft choice. This can often be valuable compensation for the player they are trading away. Rarely is a trade made of one player for another at the same position (though this did occur between two quarterbacks recently). More often a team will trade a player when they have an abundance of strength in that position for one who, they hope, will beef up a weak area; a defensive back for a wide receiver, an offensive lineman for a kicker.

The *college draft* is the method the NFL set up for professional teams to acquire the right to sign the first contract with players just ending their college days. It's a kind of monopoly "slave market" in that the players have no say in choosing their employer. You go where you are picked, or try the Canadian League.

Who gets first pick on which round becomes very complicated and at times mysterious, but at the bottom of it all is a formula designed to balance the teams of the NFL. The teams that have played the worst, as evidenced by their won/lost record of the past year, get the highest (first) choices. This should allow them to pick the best players. Of course, in the college draft they are choosing for potential, and except with certain gypsies, fortune-telling has always been a chancy proposition.

Who is a free agent? This philosophical question has troubled men almost since time began. Great minds have pondered the nuances and ramifications of this puzzle. But in football there are some absolutes. A free agent is a player who shows up at training camp and says, "I'm good. In fact, I'm the greatest. I'm so good, let me show you what I can do and you will be so dazzled you will sign me for a million dollars." The question is if he's that good, why is he a free agent? Except for players who have played out their option year, or who haven't been claimed on waivers, a free agent is often an unknown element.

A free agent is not necessarily free to the team that signs him. He is free in that he can negotiate with any team to buy his services. There is no team that "owns" him and can act as the initiating party to the trade. He is not free in that the team that acquires his services may have to compensate the team that "owned" him previously. This may be by money, draft choice, or player trade. Some free agents really are free (other than their salary). They come into training camp out of nowhere, and occasionally one will be found to be a diamond in the dust.

BETTER PLAYING THROUGH CHEMISTRY

The subject of drugs and athletics has been with us for as long as winning has been important, a long, long time. What the ancient Greek athletes used to get that extra bit of energy, or alleviate the pain and fatigue that comes from an all-out athletic effort, is unknown. Inca Indian couriers, who had to run for miles over the rocky, high-altitude Andean trails, chewed coca leaves. The cocaine in the leaves' juice masked the fatigue and numbed the body. Our athletes have the benefit of technology: amphetamines for that extra alertness and energy; novocain and procaine to numb the pain of twisted joints, broken bones, and bruised nerves; anabolic steroids for weight and muscle development—these are the tools that modern science has given the competitor in our lifetime.

The subject of drug use in our culture has a built-in bias. It is almost impossible to mention the word "drugs" without an instant reaction. Visions of "dope fiends" and "drug-crazed degenerates" running amok, destroying the foundations of family life, religion, and "the American way," are imagined by almost everyone. We do not intend to deal with the moral issues of drug use in or out of the locker room. Drugs are used in professional football and the subject is a valid one in the context of a description of the game.

Typically, there are four applications for which drugs are used by professional football players. These are: to build muscles and add weight; to alleviate pain and discomfort; to reduce swelling and inflamation; to provide an emotional and physical "charge" at game time. The drugs most commonly used for these purposes are, respectively, anabolic steroids, xylocaine and procaine, cortisone and Butazolidin, and amphetamines, commonly known as speed or crystal.

There are ethical issues raised in any discussion of drug use by professional athletes. The distinction between ethical and moral must be made. The ethical issue is whether or not such drug use is an acceptable exploitation of the player by team owners and coaches. In other words, does team management push its players to use drugs for the immediate satisfaction of team goals regardless of the long-term effects on the users? Is winning and making money the only interest of the management or does somebody care what happens to a player afterwards? There are those who ascribe a completely cynical motivation to team management, and there are others who see top management as universally benign. The truth probably lies somewhere in between.

Anabolic steroids are used in the off-season to make muscles bigger and add weight. Their use is outlawed in amateur athletics. There have been strong rumors regarding the use of steroids by the East German Olympic women's swimming teams. The East Germans deny the charges; however, there is some evidence of its use. The East German girls won everything in sight for a while and they did appear to be exceptionally well muscled, even for Teutonic womanhood. Other Eastern European athletic teams have also been accused of illegal use of steroids. American Olympians, trying to remain competitive, have employed steroids and been disqualified from competition as a result. Television's *60 Minutes* did a segment on the subject a year or two ago.

Do anabolic steroids cause physical or mental problems for their users later in life? There is a growing body of evidence that such may be the case, but we don't have a definite answer yet. We do know that there are professional football players who use them to build up their muscles and increase body weight. Football is a game of strength, size, and weight. It's one very physical game and coaches want big, strong men on their team.

Painkillers are also actively used. The motion picture *North Dallas Forty* contains a scene in which an injured running back is encouraged to let a trainer shoot him with a pain killer so he can go back in the game. He does go back in, and is permanently injured as a result. The problem with the use of xylocaine and procaine is that they mask the pain, which is the body's way of saying, "Hey, you're damaged. Stop what you are doing and let this thing heal." Masking this signal permits an injured player to stress the already injured area and exacerbate the injury. He can't feel it so he doesn't know it's damaged.

Cortisone and Butazolidin, which are anti-inflamatory agents, are often used in the same way and for the same reasons as the painkillers. Butazolidin has been banned for use on racehorses, but it is not illegal to use on people.

"Uppers," the amphetamines, known on the street as speed or crystal, are controlled substances and are available (or so the fiction goes) by prescription only. There is no doubt about the injurious long-term effects of continued amphetamine use. There are "speed freaks" in abundance all over the country as a result of the drug culture of the sixties, and there is much evidence of its abuse by professional football players.

In the late sixties and early seventies team physicians were ordering amphetamines in bulk quantities from the wholesale drug houses. Unless these were flushed down the drain, it is safe to assume that these team physicians were prescribing all this speed to the players. It was open knowledge that team members were coming out onto the field "wired" and raring to go. They couldn't sit still. The euphemism was that they were "psyched up" for the game; psyched up with the aid of modern chemistry and their friendly team doctor or trainer. There is some reason to believe that the trainers were delegated to administer the drugs.

One effect of massive doses of amphetamines is an extreme anger bordering on rage. The symptoms have been described as a temporary paranoic schizophrenia. When exhorted to go out and "kill the bastards," meant euphemistically no doubt, people in this temporary state of derangement tend to take those instructions a bit more literally. In addition, the drug taker can't feel very much pain or retains little memory of it, and hence feels invulnerable. You have only to watch the exultation on the face of a linebacker who has pushed all the blockers out of the way and thrown himself full force on the quarterback to realize that there is something unnatural in his reaction. They have been seen to jump up and down, point fingers in derision at the fallen victim, and shout imprecations. They often have to be dragged away by teammates.

Injuries abound, to the victim and the hitter as well. In 1971, as a result of costly settlements to ex-players injured as a result of such drug abuse, the league instituted new rules to curb heavy drug use. Henceforth, said the NFL, all team medication purchases must be reported to the league. They now claim that monitoring such purchases and investigating when the quantities become excessive has cured the problem. There are those who question that statement and point to the obvious loopholes in the control system. You can believe what you want.

For more on this subject, refer to *The Nightmare Season*, by Arnold J. Mandell, M.D., who spent the 1973 season as a team psychiatrist with the San Diego Chargers. He was fired in 1974. He is a prominent researcher in brain chemistry and psychopharmacology and is cochairman of the Department of Psychiatry at the University of California at San Diego Medical School.

9

Putting Your Money
Where Your Mouth Is

People will wager on almost anything. There is something universal in this compulsion. One can imagine Cro-Magnon man taking bets on how fast the ice would melt during the last glaciation of Europe. Football brings out this quality in its fans, and it is one of the major betting sports in the United States.

Wagering takes several forms. There is the dyed-in-the-wool fanatic who will bet on his team no matter what the situation may be. Putting money on his team is a gesture of support, a good luck charm. If he doesn't put a few bucks on his heroes, the charm will be broken and the team will run into bad luck. These wagers are usually small in quantity and made with supporters of the opposition or friends willing to oblige him. They know that he *must* get a bet down for his conscience's sake.

Then there are those who "need a little action" in order to enjoy the game. The "spice" is only present when there is something risked. Money is cheaper than a punch in the nose. With a bet going for him, this spectator takes a genuine interest in the goings-on on the field. These types usually bet with both the opposition supporters and with the bookies.

The third type is a gambler, that is, he tries to make money from wagering. He usually gets his money down with the professionals, the bookies. The gambler knows his football. He or she watches the *morning line,* keeps track of injuries to key players, the field and weather conditions, won/lost records and all the minutiae of records and statistics. His idea is that if you know enough, you can pick the winner. Unlike horseracing, football is predictable, or at least so the theory goes.

Football wagering is, however, quite different from betting on the nags, dogs, or how many cherries come up on a random number-generating one-armed bandit. The difference is *the spread.*

The spread is an attempt to equalize the chances for the wagerer. The spread makes the "odds" even when the teams are unequal in strength and record. The team deemed to be the stronger of the two has to score more points than the weaker team for the wagerer to win the wager. For instance, team A is considered by the experts to be nine points better than team B. If a wagerer has his money on team A, it must win by ten points or more for him to win his bet. Conversely, the gambler who has picked team B wins his bet even if his team loses—providing they lose by nine or less points. That's called beating the spread.

The bookies love the spread. They don't care who wins or loses. They make their money anyhow. A bookie gets a percentage, typically ten percent of the wager, paid by the loser. This is called the "vigorish." If a man bets ten dollars on, say, the New York Jets and loses, he pays the bookie eleven dollars. If, wonder of wonders, he wins, he collects ten dollars from the bookie. As a rule, for every winner, there is a loser. The bookie laughs all the way to the bank.

The spread for each game in the schedule is generated in that gambler's paradise of the Old West, Las Vegas. In a room at the Union Plaza on the Boulevard of Broken Dreams sits an expatriate from the mythical Eastern Kingdom of Brooklyn, one Mr. Bob Martin. Mr. Martin mulls over all the information on all the factors that enter into a team's performance on a particular day, at a particular place, in particular weather, against a particular opponent. This data gets homogenized, sanitized, and epitomized. The whole thing goes into Bob Martin's head and comes out as the *morning line* early in the week of the game. It is picked up by the wire services and major newspaper chains and given to the world. Bookies use it and the major gambling houses accept it as gospel.

During the week, the line tends to change. In the regions that support a team, regional loyalties affect the local spread. Late-developing factors such as injuries and weather forecasts are also reflected in the point spread late in the week.

One interesting aspect of the factors that go into developing the morning line is the role of emotion as a part of the weighting. According to Martin, emotion is one of the most important elements that go into his judgments. How emotionally charged up one team is and whether or not the game is on home ground are definitely factors. Another very important emotional factor is the audience. On a Monday night with a national audience watching, teams seem to "play over their heads." Statistically, over the years, the underdogs playing at home have beat the spread far beyond the expected probability.

The betting experts also say that the team with the best defense is going to win. It appears that the coaches who build NFL teams agree with this point of view. Many of them emphasize defense and build the offense after the defense has been put together.

The moral of this is, if you want to support your team and make a buck or two, stay away from the big point spreads and keep your eyes on the teams with the best defense.

10

The Season to Be Jolly

To the avid football fan the year begins in August and ends in January, or possibly the first weekend in February. The rest of the year is that interminable period called "the off-season" as if it were not quite wholesome.

In August the pre-season begins—four games scheduled in August that "don't count." However, the fans still have to pay to watch. They can be intraconference or interconference. The feeling is that some are scheduled in the hope of exploiting natural rivalries that cannot find expression during the regular season. Given their geography, there exists a natural rivalry between the Oakland Raiders and the San Francisco 49ers; given their places in the Western Divisions of the AFC and NFC, they never play each other during the regular season. So, the NFL has scheduled a pre-season game between these two teams for a number of years.

The season "counts." The season is where the stats come from, where the standings come from, and what counts toward the playoffs.

The season consists of sixteen games. Eight of these are a round-robin series within the division, at home and away (the other guy's home), for the divisions consisting of five teams. In both the National and American Conferences two divisions are of five teams and one is of four teams. In the divisions of only four teams, this round robin yields six games, so they play an additional game against each of the two fifth-place teams in their conference (at home and away—a total of four more). The remaining games in the season are a mixture of interconference (as many as four, as few as two) games and intraconference (four) games, weighted by the standing of the team at the end of last year's season. If you're low in the standings you tend to play other teams that were low in the standings. If you won a lot, you play other winners. A poor team plays an easy season; a good team plays a hard season. But last year's standings don't always reflect this year's ability. A poor team that has suddenly improved, playing an easy season, can end up in the playoffs. If they are then up against a good team that has played a hard season, the result is a foregone conclusion, isn't it? Maybe, maybe not, which is why some people bet on the games. Maybe the "poor" team is better than anyone suspected, and who knows, given their "easy" season.

The post-season is everything that comes after the season ends in the latter part of December. This includes the wild-card games, the playoffs, the Super Bowl and the Pro Bowl.

What is a wild-card team? There are two of them, one from each conference. In each conference there are three divisions; however, to have a play-down to determine the top team in the conference, you need four teams. The wild-card team is that fourth team. They are determined in a wild-card game between the two teams that did not end up at the top of their division, but in their conference as a whole ended up with the best record (won/lost) for second place. Since there is a possibility that all three (or more) second-place teams can tie in their won/lost record for the season, the league has worked out rules for breaking ties. They start with won/lost records in conference games, proceed through won/lost records in "common" games, best net points in conference games, then in all games. If a tie still exists, the next consideration is the strength of the season of each team. This is followed by the net touchdowns each team scored. Finally, if the teams are still tied in their records, a coin is tossed. Similar tie-breaking rules can be used to determine end-of-season standings, if needed. The winners of the wild-card game become the wild-card team for their conference in the playoffs.

Now comes the most intensive weekend in football. There are four games in one weekend, all televised: two on Saturday, which is rare for pro football, and two on Sunday. Out of this ferment emerge four victorious teams. The next round of the playoffs is played one week later with both games on Sunday. The league at this point prays that one of the home teams will be from the East Coast and the other from the West Coast so one game can be played at noon (EST) and the other at 4:00 (EST). No matter where the two home teams are located, both games will be shown on TV in their entirety. If both teams are located in the central part of our country this could create a weird scheduling of the games as far as the home fans who will be attending the games in person are concerned, with one game starting at 11:00 in the morning and the other at 3:00 in the afternoon. Or if they both were on the West Coast, one would start at 9:00 in the morning. TV is where the money is, so the games are scheduled for TV, not the attending fans.

After these two playoffs, there are two champions, one from the AFC and one from the NFC, each regarded as the best from their conference. Now it's time for the Super Bowl, played at least two weeks after the last playoff game (usually the third week in January).

THE SUPER BOWL! The game of the best against the best. The game that determines who is *really* the best. The game that determines the World Champions. A kind of insanity infects the country the week before this game, but it most particularly invades three cities, the two that have teams playing in the Super Bowl and the city where the Super Bowl is to be played. Any city can bid to have the Super Bowl, but the league officials have a bias for cities in the Sunbelt. Who wants a Super Bowl in a howling blizzard with the temperature (including wind chill factor) at −40°F.? However, if more cities build covered stadiums, you may yet see the Super Bowl in Seattle or Minnesota.

The winners of the Super Bowl are the World Champions (no matter that the only teams involved are from the United States). The owner of a Super Bowl ring has tangible proof that he has been publicly acknowledged as "the best." The glory covers everyone who has played in the Super Bowl, even those who have played and lost. To have played and won makes a player a part of the "elect." These are football's finest. These are our gladiators. They have the physical strength, skill, and cunning to have survived and come out on top. Just as the gladiators of ancient Rome who could survive in the arena were held in great esteem and were heroes to the populous, these are our heroes.

The final game is the Pro Bowl, almost anticlimactic for the fans after the Super Bowl, but important to the players themselves. The Pro Bowl is an all-star game. To be chosen to play in the Pro Bowl, a player is acknowledged by the experts to be among the best personally, not just as a member of a team. He is the best of all the best receivers, or linemen, or kickers playing football. To be chosen All-Pro is an honor, and adds to his monetary value as a player as well. The Pro Bowl has an additional monetary value to all the players of football; the proceeds go to the pension fund of the Players Association. This game pits the AFC against the NFC just as the Super Bowl does, but here the effort is to mesh a group of individuals into a cohesive group very quickly. A Super Bowl team has been playing together all year and they know each other and how they work together. The Pro Bowl teams must learn to do that in just one week. This game is usually played the last week in January and thus ends the football year. After the Pro Bowl there is, for true football fans, nothing to do or watch until the next year begins in August.

Glossary

Audible. A verbal call by the quarterback to change the play while his team is lined up on the line of scrimmage. He alerts his team with a predesignated signal and then calls the numbers to indicate what new play is being called. This usually occurs if the defense has lined up in an unanticipated formation.

Back judge. See **Officials.**

Balanced attack. When a team is able to move the ball effectively by passing and running, they have a balanced attack. With the threat of either a pass or a run on any play, the defense is forced into the position of trying to cope with both. If a team is known to be particularly strong in one, but not the other, the defense can anticipate and be prepared to defend against that strength.

Balanced line. When there are an equal number of offensive linemen on each side of the center.

Ball control. A technique used by pro teams in the last minutes of the game to protect a lead. A team is "controlling the ball" when they are stressing running plays in an effort to keep the ball moving down the field. Passes, if used, are generally short and used to gain enough yardage for a first down. All of this is aimed at keeping the clock running so the other team cannot gain possession of the ball with time left to score again.

Blind-sided. When a player is hit from an angle that did not allow him to see the approaching defensive player, he has been blind-sided. Knee and ankle injuries often result because the player has not been able to prepare for the hit and has his cleats firmly planted in the turf.

Blitzing (or **red dogging**). A defensive play in which one or more players in the defensive secondary charge across the line of scrimmage at the snap of the ball. The purpose is to knock down or immobilize the quarterback for a loss of yardage. Because much of the defense is now across the line of scrimmage it can leave them vulnerable to draws and screens. When it works it can cause a turnover (because the quarterback fumbles) but most usually results in a large loss of yardage.

Blocked kick. A kick has been blocked if its flight is obstructed by a member of the defensive team after it has been kicked. The ball is then free and can be carried for a gain in yardage by whichever team recovers it. The exception to this rule is a PAT conversion attempt. In this case, when the ball is blocked, it's dead.

Blocking. Contact by an offensive player on a defensive player. He can use any part of his body except his hands. Tripping is also a no-no.

Blocking back. An offensive back used primarily as a blocker. He rarely carries the ball.

Bomb. A long pass usually thrown by the quarterback to a wide receiver. When it works, a long gain or a touchdown may be at the end of the play. But it's a gamble, and if it goes bad, the best that can be expected is an incomplete pass. The worst is an interception.

Bootleg. A play used in short yardage situations where the quarterback fakes a handoff to the back going around the end of the line. The quarterback actually keeps the ball and tries to run with it around the other end. Because the quarterback is too valuable to be injured for the sake of a few yards and is not expected to be one of the better runners on a team, deception to draw the defense to the wrong end of the line is an important part of the play. It is used primarily when there is only short yardage needed.

Broken field running (or **open field running**). When a running back has passed the line of scrimmage and there are relatively few defenders between him and the goal line. This is where fancy footwork can come into play and where the beauty and grace of the running game is showcased.

Broken pattern. When a pass receiver has not run the route called by the quarterback.

Brushing block. A block by an offensive player at less than the full impact possible. It is used by backs and tight ends before going out on a pass route. It is sometimes used to mislead the defense into believing that a receiver is going out for a pass. It is also used to set up a defender for another block by another offensive player.

Bullet pass. A hard, straight pass. There is less chance of an interception on a pass that is thrown hard. If it is too hard, however, the receiver may not be able to hold onto it.

Button hook. See **Hook.**

Chain (or **yardage chain**). A metal chain that is ten yards long and is attached to two long poles. It is used to measure for first downs.

Chain gang. Those persons responsible for the yardage chain. They place and hold it on the sideline, and under the direction of the head linesman bring the chain onto the field for actual measurements.

Chuck (also called **bump and run**). A hit by a defensive back on a potential pass receiver. It is designed to delay the receiver or force him out of his designated route. It can be used only once and only within the first five yards of the run.

Clipping. A block on a defensive player from his rear. This is a personal foul and results in a fifteen-yard penalty. Sometimes a defender will turn his back on the opposing player just as he is about to be blocked. If an official sees this action he is unlikely to call a clipping infraction.

Clotheslining. A defensive player swinging an arm out at the head or neck of an offensive player running past him is called clotheslining. It is now illegal. The name comes from the fact that the hit player reacts as if he had run into a neck-high clothesline.

College draft. A method set up by the NFL to share the wealth of talent coming out of the colleges each year. The intention is to even out the chances of signing good player material equally among all teams. The teams with the worst records have the first shot at signing a rookie. The rookie has no bargaining power regarding which team he can play for.

Conversion (or **PAT**). The attempt to score a point after a touchdown. A placekick is almost always used, however, the ball legally could be carried or thrown over the goal line. If the ball is kicked, it must go over the crossbar and between the uprights of the goalpost. The play begins from the 2-yard line and the ball cannot be kicked from closer than that line.

Cornerback. A defensive back who lines up outside the safety and corner linebacker. He usually covers the wide receiver and is probably among the fastest runners on the defensive team.

Count. The word or number in the signal system on which the ball will be snapped and the offense begins play. The count is varied to prevent anticipation on the part of the defense, who can be drawn offsides at times if the quarterback switches to a long count without altering the original cadence.

Counter play. An offensive backfield action in which the flow of the play moves in one direction while the ballcarrier moves across the line in the opposite direction. See also **Going against the grain** and **Reverse.**

Coverage. The methods of defending against the pass and the type of assignments in the defensive secondary. Man-to-man coverage, zone coverage, or a combination may be used by a team.

Crawling. An attempt to advance the ball after an official has blown it dead. A five-yard penalty is supposed to result. However, in pro football, where a ballcarrier can get up and continue running if he has slipped untouched, it is rarely called.

Cross-body block. An offensive block in which the blocker throws himself in front of the defender. He shoves his side (arm, shoulder, and ribs) against the upper legs of the defender. With luck and good conditioning he blocks out his man without crippling himself.

Crossing pattern. Two receivers cross each other's path downfield at a predesignated point. They could be two wide receivers, a wide receiver and a tight end, or any other combination of running backs. The intention is to confuse the defense sufficiently to allow one of the receivers to break free.

Crowding the receiver. Tight coverage of the receiver by the defender without contact being made.

Cup. See **Pocket.**

Cutback. See **Counter play** and **Going against the grain.**

Cutdown. A player has been cut down when he is the victim of a body block. A cutdown is a low block (below the waist) whether it is a shoulder block or a cross body block. The victim of a high block has been "creamed" or "run over."

Cut-off block. A move by an offensive player who is between the ballcarrier and a defender, used to prevent the defender from moving laterally. The move does not have to be an actual block but merely has to cut off the defender's movement.

Dead ball. The ball is dead after the play has been whistled over by an official.

Deep man (or **long man,** also **deep receiver**). The receiver that is furthest downfield in a pass pattern.

Defensive holding. Illegal use of the hands by a defensive player. It can be called any time a defensive player holds on to the shirt of an offensive player and refuses to release him. The penalty is five yards and a first down.

Delay. See **Draw play.**

Delay of game. The offensive team must snap the ball within thirty seconds of the time the referee declares the ball in play. If the play doesn't get off in time the penalty is five yards.

Delay pass. A pass pattern in which the potential receiver, usually a tight end, blocks or fakes a block before running his pass route. This is a deception play designed to make the defender believe a receiver is not going out on a pass route.

Dive. A running play in which the back lines up almost directly opposite a potential hole in the line and runs straight into it with no faking. The success of the play depends on the quickness of the handoff, the line's ability to make a hole, and the back's ability to cut if the hole doesn't materialize.

Double coverage. Two defenders assigned to cover one pass receiver when he runs his pass route. Usually one will guard him short and the other long. The short defender will often "chuck" the receiver as he leaves the line of scrimmage to attempt to force him to alter his route and disrupt the timing between the receiver and the quarterback.

Double team blocking. When two offensive players are assigned to block the same defensive player. The double team block is likely to use a lineman and a back to block one defensive lineman. A brush block by one offensive player to set up a full block by another is also considered double team blocking.

Double wing formation. An offensive formation in which a player is positioned just outside and behind the offensive tackle on the weak side of the line. The player is usually a blocking back, but he can be a receiver sent in to replace one running back. The advantage of the double wing is the speed with which the wingback can get downfield; the weakness is that only one back remains behind the quarterback. The weakness outrules the strength; this is rarely seen in pro ball.

Down. A unit of action in the game, one full play. A team has four opportunities (downs) to move the ball ten yards forward from the original line of scrimmage. A down starts with the snap of the ball and ends when the play is whistled dead. If a team moves the ball ten yards downfield during the course of the four downs while retaining possession of the ball they have gained a first down. They then have another four chances to move the ball another ten yards.

Down-and-in. Any pass route that requires the receiver to run straight downfield and then cut in toward the middle of the field.

Down-and-out. Any pass route that requires the receiver to run straight downfield, then cut toward the outside or sidelines.

Downfield. To the offensive team, any area on the other side of the line of scrimmage in the opposition's territory.

Downfield block. Any block thrown by an offensive player beyond the line of scrimmage. Generally more difficult to do than a block on the line of scrimmage.

Draw play (or **delay**). A running play, designed to look like a pass play, intended to draw the defense across the line of scrimmage to rush the passer. The quarterback drops back as if to pass and then hands off to a running back who carries the ball. The offensive line sets up as it would on a pass play and then tries to draw the defense to one side or the other. The running back goes through wherever an opening develops. The draw play can be particularly effective against a blitz and can help slow down the pass rush.

Dropkick. Any kick where the kicker drops the ball and kicks it the instant it hits the ground. You don't see this much anymore. The forward pass obsoleted the dropkick a long time ago.

Eating the football. When the quarterback, behind the line of scrimmage, deliberately decides to take a loss rather than throw the ball and risk an interception. He hangs on to the ball and take his lumps. He has been "sacked."

Eligible receiver. Any of five players on the offensive team legally entitled to receive a forward pass. The two ends and three backfield men are eligible. Only rarely will an interior lineman be eligible, and this is if he is the outermost man on either side of the line. The quarterback is an eligible receiver; however, he cannot receive a pass he has thrown.

Ends. The men who line up on either end of the offensive line. They are eligible to catch a forward pass and are lined up as a tight end or a split end.

End around. A running play with the end carrying the ball around the end of the line. See also **Power sweep.**

End line. The last line at each end of the field. The end of the end zone. The line on which the goalpost is situated.

End zone. The ten yards between the goal line and the end line (between the goal line and the goalposts).

Extra point. See **Conversion.**

Face guarding. The deliberate obstruction of receiver's vision by a defensive guard who puts his hands or waves his arms in front of the receiver's face. The penalty for this infraction is a first down at the point the infraction occurred.

Face masking. Grabbing a player by his face mask to delay him or bring down the ball carrier. A very dangerous practice that has resulted in serious injury. A fifteen-yard penalty if the official sees it.

Fade back. The retreat back from the line of scrimmage by the quarterback as he moves into position to pass the ball. This gives him sufficient time to find an open receiver and throw the ball.

Fair catch. When the receiver of a punt feels that he will not be able to advance the ball, he can call for a fair catch by raising one hand high in the air. The next play begins at the point he catches the ball. Once he signals, the defense cannot make contact with him without being penalized. The receiver must, however, catch the ball. If he fumbles, the ball is free and the other team can recover.

Field goal. A scrimmage play that results in a kick which travels over the crossbar and between the uprights of the goalpost. The ball may be either placekicked or drop-kicked (today it is always placekicked). A field goal is worth three points.

Field judge. See **Officials.**

Fill. When a back fills a hole by blocking a defensive lineman not blocked by the offensive lineman. The back usually fills for a guard moving off to prepare for a trap block or leading a sweep run.

Finesse. A deception tactic designed to pull one or more defenders in the wrong direction by means other than physical force. Meanwhile, the play goes in the opposite direction.

First down. Gaining ten yards. A first down provides four opportunities to gain the next ten yards. Once the ball has moved ten more yards the team has a new first down.

Flag. The penalty marker thrown by an official to indicate an infraction has occurred. It is a bright dayglow yellow handkerchief stowed in the back pocket of the officials. You will hear such terms as, "There's a flag on the play" or "There are flags flying all over the field." Also: the four flags that mark the four corners of the field.

Flag route. A pass play in which the receiver heads for the flag that marks the corner of the end zone. This play can result in heart-stopping touchdowns and interceptions.

Flank. An area that begins several yards outside the tight end and extends to the sidelines. The area in which the flanker lines up and where the sweep or flare (swing) pass is directed.

Flanker. An offensive player who is positioned outside his own tight end and one yard behind the line of scrimmage. He is technically a running or blocking back, but is often used as a receiver because of his ability to get downfield quickly.

Flare pass (or **swing pass**). A pass thrown behind the line of scrimmage to a back running toward the sideline. The receiver in this case is expected to gain yardage after he has caught the ball.

Flood. When two or more receivers are sent into one area of the defensive secondary. Used primarily in an attempt to neutralize the effectiveness of the zone defense.

Flood formation. A formation designed to allow a team to get several receivers downfield quickly. Sometimes called a "triple" since three receivers line up on one side of the field.

Flow. The direction in which the play moves, either left or right. The backs may move in one direction to draw the defense, while the ballcarrier moves in the opposite direction "against the flow."

Fly (or **streak**). A pass route in which the wide receiver runs downfield as fast as possible in an effort to get behind the defender. There is little deception in this play.

Footsteps (or **hearing footsteps**). A term used when the receiver is preparing to be hit by an approaching defender. He often misses the catch as a result of his attention not being focused on the ball.

Forward motion (or **forward progress**). The point at which the ballcarrier's downfield progress is stopped and the ball is declared dead. Also movement downfield as compared to lateral or backward movement.

Forward pass. Any pass thrown by a member of the offense that travels downfield and lands closer to the goal line than the point from which it was thrown.

Forward wall. The five offensive linemen: the center, the two guards, and the two tackles.

Foul (or **infraction**). Any violation of a playing rule that leads to a penalty.

Free agent. In pro football, any player who is not drafted or traded, but who signs a contract and is given an opportunity to make the team. Also: one who has played out his option year and is free to accept offers from other teams, or has been released on waivers.

Free kick. Any kick during which the receiving team may not rush or otherwise interfere with the kicker. This includes kickoffs, a kick after a safety, and a kick after a fair catch. The last is very unusual and would probably be a field goal attempt. The receiving team would be given possession of the ball as after a punt or field goal attempt.

Free safety. The safety not assigned to cover a specific offensive player, the free safety is usually the deepest man in the defensive backfield. Most often it is the weak-side safety who is free, but it can be the safety on the strong side.

Frequency chart. Every play, alignment, and formation used by both the offense and the defense is noted and charted by the opposition. The frequency with which a team reacts to a specific situation with a particular action is noted. The information is used in an attempt to anticipate the actions of that team and to formulate new plays. Blitzing or pass plays on particular downs are examples of plays that might show up on frequency charts.

Front four. The two defensive tackles and the two defensive ends. Often given a nickname by fans or broadcasters— The Steel Curtain, The Orange Crush.

Full house. A term used when the offensive backfield lines up in the traditional T formation with three set backs behind the quarterback and between the offensive tackles.

Fullback. In the traditional T formation the fullback lines up three to four yards directly behind the quarterback. He is often the biggest offensive player on the field and is used primarily to block or to carry the ball directly over the middle.

Fumble. When the ballcarrier loses the ball before the play is over. The ball is then "loose" and can be recovered by any player on either team and the play continue. If the defense recovers it's a turnover, since possession has changed.

Game plan. The predetermined plan of action for each team. It is worked out by the coaches after viewing game films of the upcoming opponent. It considers any weakness that has been spotted, and is designed to deal with the style and patterns of play in the opponent's past performance. Though a team will attempt to follow the game plan as closely as possible, adjustments have to be made to cope with new strategy or tactics introduced by the opposition in the actual game itself.

Games (or **tricks, stunts,** or **deals**). Defensive tactics that require several linemen or linebackers to exchange assignments after the snap of the ball. Because this is a deception tactic to confuse the offensive linemen, the defense lines up in normal position and tries not to telegraph their moves until the ball is snapped.

Gang tackling. Two or more defensive players tackling the ballcarrier at the same tine. This is a sign of aggressive play and good pursuit by the defending team.

Gap. The space between two offensive or defensive linemen. The positions assigned to offensive linemen create "gaps" in the line. Defensive linemen will line up in the middle of that gap and attempt to "shoot the gap" if the split becomes too wide.

Gap defense. A defensive formation where all the defensive lineman are lined up in the gaps between the offensive linemen. Usually used in short yardage situations.

Goal line. The line separating the playing field from the end zone. The imaginary "vertical plane" that must be penetrated to score a touchdown. Once it is crossed, a touchdown is scored even if the ballcarrier is pushed back across the line.

Goalposts. The contraption at the end of each end zone that now looks like a broadened Y and used to look like an H. The uprights are 18 feet 6 inches apart and the crossbar 10 feet above the ground. In a successful field goal or PAT conversion the ball must travel over the crossbar and between the uprights.

Going against the grain. When the ballcarrier runs in a direction opposite to the one almost everyone else is running. This can be a preset part of the play or can occur as the play develops.

Grab and shake. Since a defensive lineman can use his hands and an offensive lineman cannot, the tactic of grab and shake is designed to take that advantage. The defender, at the snap of the ball, grabs the offensive lineman by the shoulders, gives him a push to the side (one or the other), and tries to move past the offensive lineman on the same side as he reacts to the other side.

Gridiron. A term for the football playing field. Rarely used by those actually involved in the game, except historically or facetiously. It comes from the resemblance of the lines on the field to an iron rack for broiling food over a fire.

Grounding. When a passer deliberately throws away the ball in an attempt to avoid a loss of yardage when he is about to be sacked. This is a deliberate incomplete pass because there is no receiver in a position to catch the ball. The penalty is ten yards and loss of a down.

Guard. The two offensive linemen on either side of the center.

Gun shy. When after a player has been injured or hit particularly hard on a play and he pulls back so as to avoid heavy contact, he is described as gun shy. No one admits to being gun shy.

Half the distance. A penalty calling for moving the ball half the distance to the goal line. Also: a penalty given to the defensive team that is reduced to half the distance to the goal line. For example, if clipping is called on the twelve-yard line, though the penalty is fifteen yards, it is reduced to six yards and the ball is spotted on the six-yard line.

Halfbacks. The two running backs lined up on either side of the fullback in a T formation. A halfback is usually smaller and faster than the fullback. A defensive halfback is the college equivalent of the pro cornerback.

Halftime. The fifteen-period between the two halves of the game.

Hand fighter. When a defensive lineman uses his hands to fend off an offensive blocker to make a tackle or to get at a passer, he is a hand fighter.

Handoff. One offensive player giving the ball to another offensive player. The ball is handed to the other person, not thrown.

Hang time. The relative time a ball spends in the air when it has been kicked. A long hang time gives the kicking team an advantage since it gives them a lot of time to get downfield to defend against the run back.

Hash marks. The set of lines placed a little over 23.5 yards (70 feet 9 inches exactly) in from the sidelines. They mark each yard of the field with a short line. If a play ends between the hash marks and the sidelines, the ball is moved in and spotted on the hash marks for the next play.

Head linesman. See **Officials.**

Head-up blocking. A blocking play by a member of the offense trying to protect his quarterback. The offensive lineman moves forward from his crouch position, arms folded, into the defensive player in an attempt to drive him back (or at least stop his forward momentum) by sheer weight and strength.

High-low block (or **tackles**). When two players are involved in blocking or tackling an opponent and one hits him high, the other low.

Holding.

Offensive. Usually occurs when the offense has to "buy some time" to get off a play. The rules hold that an offensive blocker may not (1) encircle with his arms, (2) touch the head, neck, and other areas above the shoulders, nor (3) block below the knees any defensive player. The poor offensive soul looks deformed, since he may not move his hands beyond the vertical plane of his elbows.

The rules do provide him with some freedom of movement: If the defender is trying to grab his jersey, arms, shoulders, or unmentionables, the offensive blocker is permitted to move his arms up and down to ward off the unsolicited advances.

Defensive. The rules are complex and mysterious. The infraction breaks into two separate situations: holding during a chucking situation, and holding during other times. The former can occur only in the first five yards beyond the line of scrimmage during an expected pass play. In this situation the defender can hit (block) the potential receiver but may not (1) encircle, (2) do what is mentioned in (2) and (3) of offensive holding, nor (3) grab the jersey of his opponent. Other times the rules boil down to the idea that a defensive player may use his hands to protect himself and that is all. Obviously, this is one of the infractions that require the wisdom of Solomon or a Supreme Court Judge. The rules on holding are so complex and detailed that you have to accept the official's judgment.

Hook (or **buttonhook**). A pass route in which the receiver runs downfield, then suddenly stops and turns to face the quarterback. Timing is essential because the quarterback usually releases the ball before the receiver turns. He may have to take a few steps back up the field to catch the ball as it approaches.

Hook and go. A pass route in which the receiver runs a hook pattern, then, after hesitating to draw the defender toward him, breaks quickly downfield looking for a long pass.

I formation. An offensive formation where two or three backs line up directly behind the quarterback.

Illegal forward pass. A pass thrown after the quarterback has crossed the line of scrimmage; a pass thrown to an ineligible receiver; a pass that doesn't go in a forward direction.

Illegal Procedure. Movement by any member of the offensive line after the team is "set." Once the offensive lineman places his hand on the ground, he may not move. An illegal movement can be in any direction except across the line of scrimmage. Movement across the line of scrimmage is not illegal procedure, but an offside infraction.

In motion. The movement by an eligible receiver parallel to or angled back from the line of scrimmage before the ball is snapped.

Ineligible receiver. An interior offensive lineman may not go downfield before the pass is thrown, nor may he touch a forward pass. They are ineligible to receive the ball. The penalty is fifteen yards.

Influence block. Partial contact by an offensive player on a defender, designed to set up the defender for a full block by another offensive player.

Infraction (or foul). Any action by either team that violates one of the playing rules and results in a penalty.

Inside. A term used to describe the movement of the offensive receivers. If, while running his pass route, he breaks toward the center of the field, he is moving to the inside. If he breaks toward the sidelines, he is moving to the outside. Also: an informal term to describe the area between the two offensive tackles.

Intentional grounding. See **Grounding.**

Interception. A pass, intended for an offensive player, caught by a defensive player. When a pass has been thrown it can be caught by an eligible receiver on the offensive team or by any defensive player. The defender who catches the ball can return it as far as he can. This is a turnover and the defending team now has possession of the ball. An interception is one of two times (the other is a fumble recovered by the defense) when the ball changes possession other than after a fourth down, punt, or a score.

Keeper. A play in which the quarterback retains possession of the ball and runs with it himself. Usually in short yardage situations.

Keying (or **reading**). Keying is the method of anticipating the opposition's tactic. Particular opposition players are observed and their actions interpreted. It is important for the quarterback to read the defense and determine their pass coverage. For the defense, it is important (typically) for the free safety to read the intentions of the offensive backfield.

Kickoff. A free kick at the beginning of the game, and at the beginning of the second half. Also used to turn over the ball after touchdowns and field goals.

Kicking tee. A device used to hold the football in an upright position to permit the kicker to kickoff without anyone holding the ball. The tee is usually used only at the kickoff at the beginning of each half and after scoring.

Lateral (or **pitch**). A toss at right angles to, or backward from, the direction of the play. It can be thrown anywhere on the field. If the catch is fumbled the defense can recover, but cannot advance the ball. A lateral may be part of a pre-designed play or may just develop as a reaction to defensive moves. A lateral pass becomes a forward pass if it ends up closer to the goal line than the point from which it was thrown. It could then be an illegal forward pass.

Line judge. See **Officials.**

Line of scrimmage. An imaginary line stretching from sideline to sideline through the middle of the ball as the play begins. The offensive and defensive lines take positions on either side of the line of scrimmage to start each play. The gain or loss of the play is measured from the line of scrimmage. Often simply "the line."

Linebacker. A defensive player who lines up behind the line of scrimmage behind the lineman. He is part of the defensive secondary. In short yardage situations, his primary responsibility is to stop the runner. In pass plays his responsibility is to cover the receiver. Often blitzes and fills holes in the line.

Linesman (or **head linesman**). See **Officials**.

Live color. A color predesignated as the signal for an audible. There may be more than one and they may be changed during the.course of the game.

Loft. A long, high pass that allows the receiver time to get downfield and under the reception point. Compare to bullet pass.

Log block. When a trapping offensive lineman blocks his man to the inside rather than attempting to drive him out beyond the hole. Used against hard-charging defensive linemen who close the hole quickly.

Long man. See **Deep man**.

Look-in. A quick pass over the center, usually immediately after the quarterback has taken the snap from the center. It describes any play in which the receiver breaks downfield and then quickly cuts to the inside.

Loose ball. A ball in play, but not in the possession of any player. It is a free ball and can be recovered by any player on either team.

Man-head-on (or **man-on-nose**). When a defensive player is lined up on the line of scrimmage exactly opposite an offensive lineman.

Man in motion. See **In motion**.

Man-to-man coverage. A type of coverage in the defensive secondary in which each defender is assigned to a specific receiver. In the usual assignment the cornerbacks cover the wide receivers, the strong safety covers the tight end, the weak-side safety will either cover a set back or remain free, and the linebackers cover the set backs.

Middle linebacker. The linebacker in the middle of the defensive line facing the offensive center in the traditional 4 – 3 defense formation. There are two middle linebackers in the 3 – 4 formation.

Morning line. The point spread as determined by Bob Martin in Las Vegas and published throughout the country.

Multiple foul. Two or more infractions committed by the same team on the same down.

Multiple offense. An offensive attack where many different offensive formations are used. The purpose is to use the best formation for a particular play. It also keeps the defense guessing (or is supposed to).

MVP (most valuable player). That player chosen by a panel of sportswriters as having made the greatest contribution to his team winning a particular game.

Near back. The offensive back positioned on the side of the line where the play is designed to go. The back on the other side of the line is the far back.

Neutral zone. The area between the offensive and defensive lines on the line of scrimmage. Its width is the length of the football.

Officials. For more information on the officials, see Chapter Seven.

Back judge. Operates on the same side of the field as the line judge in a downfield position. He counts the number of defensive players on the field. He concentrates on the path of the end or the back. He rules from the deep position on holding or illegal use of the hands and on defensive infractions committed by the guarding player. He makes decisions on catching, recovery, out of bounds on his side of the field, and illegal touching of a loose ball beyond the line of scrimmage. He calls clipping on punt returns. He and the field judge are on the goal line and are responsible for ruling on the success of field goal attempts. He also rules on plays involving the pass receiver, including the legality of the catch and pass interference.

Field judge. Operates in a position deeper downfield than the back judge, usually on the tight end's side of the field. He concentrates on the tight end. He covers kicks from the line of scrimmage, passes crossing the defensive goal line, and loose balls. He calls pass interference, fair catch infractions, and clipping on kick returns when the end line is involved. With the back judge he rules on the success of field goal attempts. He times the intervals between the plays on the thirty second clock, and the intermission between halves.

Head linesman. Has the primary responsibility for ruling on offsides, encroachments, and actions pertaining to the line of scrimmage. He has the responsibility for ruling on sideline plays on his side. The linesman helps determine the forward progress of a play down the middle or on his side of the field. With the referee he is responsible for keeping track of the number of downs and is in charge of the chain gang. He also rules on actions involving receivers on his side. He calls pass interference. He rules on the legality of blockers and defenders on plays involving a ballcarrier.

Line judge. Keeps the time of the game as a backup for the clock operator. He is responsible for recording the charged time-outs, the winner of the coin toss, and the score. His position at the beginning of a play is on the line of scrimmage on the opposite side from the linesman. Along with him, the line judge is responsible for observing actions pertaining to the line of scrimmage for infractions prior to or at the snap. He rules whether a pass goes forward or backward. He also rules on whether the passer has crossed the line of scrimmage when he throws the ball. On punts he determines that only the end men move down the field before the kick is made and rules on whether the kick crosses the line. He observes the legality of the action of the members of the kicking team as they move downfield to cover the kick.

Referee. Oversees and controls the game. He gives the signals for all the fouls and is the final authority for all rule interpretations. His position is in the backfield, usually on the right side (if the quarterback is right-handed). He determines the legality of the snap and watches the deep backs for legal motion. On running plays he watches the quarterback during and after the handoff until the action clears away, then switches his attention to the runner. When the runner is downed he determines the point of forward progress and adjusts the final position of the ball. On pass plays he drops back with the quarterback and watches for legal blocks by the near linemen. As the defenders approach the quarterback, the referee concentrates on the quarterback himself. He rules on possible roughing the passer, and if the ball gets loose, rules on fumbles and incomplete passes. In kicking situations, the referee is responsible for ruling on contact by a defender on the kicker.

Side judge. Operates on the same side of the field as the linesman in a deep position. He concentrates on the path of the end or back, observing the legality of his blocks and actions taken against him. The line judge has responsibility for decisions involving the sidelines on his side of the field. He makes decisions concerning catching, recovery, or illegal touching of a loose ball beyond the line of scrimmage.

Umpire. Has responsibility for rulings on the players' equipment and their conduct and actions on the line of scrimmage. He watches for the legality of contact by the offensive linemen while blocking, and defensive players fending off the blockers. He calls rule infractions by either the offense or defense. In passing situations he follows the potential receiver, looking for illegal chucks (more than one hit within five yards of the line or any hit past that five yards). The umpire assists in ruling on incomplete or trapped pass situations when the ball is overthrown or short.

Offset defense. A defensive formation in which one of the defensive tackles (usually the weak-side tackle) lines up in the gap between the offensive guard and the center. It is a variation of the 4 – 3 defense used to strengthen the defense against the strong side of the offense.

Offside penalty. Movement by any player, either offense or defense, across the line of scrimmage before the ball is snapped. The penalty is five yards.

One-on-one. Any situation in which an offensive player and a defensive player engage against one another without any help from a teammate. This can occur in any area of the playing field.

Onside kick. A short kickoff attempted in the hope that the kicking team will be able to recover the ball and retain possession. The ball must travel at least ten yards. It is a free ball and can be recovered by either team. It is usually attempted by a team that needs another score in the closing minutes of the game. It is a gamble since if not recovered by the kicking team, the other team gains possession in the middle of the field. (See also **Squib.**)

Open field. An area downfield from the line of scrimmage.

Open field running. See **Broken field running.**

Open set. An offensive formation noted for versatility, it can be used for either running plays or passes. It is characterized by a flanker positioned wide and behind the tight end, and two running backs on either side of the quarterback.

Option blocking. Blocking for running plays in which the offensive lineman charges into the defensive player and blocks him no matter which direction he goes. Contrast this to a situation that requires that the defender be blocked in a specific direction. An option block is often used when the defender does not have to be actually moved but merely kept in contact long enough for the back to run past him.

Option pass (or **quarterback option**). A play in which the quarterback can choose to keep the ball and run it himself or pass the ball to a running back. Great if your quarterback is young, strong, and has knees that still allow him to run with any kind of speed. This play is probably seen more often in college ball than pro ball. The advantage of this play is that the quarterback does not have to choose his move until the defense has committed itself.

Option running. When the running back is given the option of running any place a hole develops. It is used in conjunction with option blocking by the offensive line. Sometimes called "pick a hole."

Outside. The area between the tight end and the sidelines on one end of the line, and between the weakside tackle and the sidelines on the other end.

Over the top. The attempt by a running back to throw himself over the offensive and defensive lines to get a first down or touchdown. Used when a short, short distance is needed (". . . they have inches to go!"). It is a dramatic play.

Overshift. A defensive formation in which the linemen set themselves strongly to one side of the center. Usually used to counter a strongly set offensive line.

Pass interference. The illegal action of a player that keeps an eligible man from getting to or catching a forward pass. It can be called on either the offense or defense. An eligible receiver on either team has an equal right to catch the ball. The penalty for defensive interference is a first down at the point of the foul. The penalty for offensive interference is fifteen yards back from the line of scrimmage.

Pass pattern. A combination of pass routes by receivers. A pass route is run by each individual receiver. A pass pattern involves two or more receivers and includes the faking moves made to evade defenders.

Pass protection. The action of keeping the defensive players away from the passer (usually the quarterback) until he has had time to throw the ball. See also **Quick pass protection.**

PAT. See **Conversion.**

Penalty marker. See **Flag.**

Personal foul. An act of illegal agression against another player. Personal fouls can be called for such acts as unnecessary roughness, clipping, piling on, hitting (with fists), kicking, and running over the passer or kicker. This last is a judgment call by the official since a defending player running with momentum can have trouble stopping. The usual penalty is fifteen yards.

Pick. When one receiver attempts to get into a position that prevents a defender from covering another receiver. On a pass, downfield blocking is not permitted, but in running his route a receiver may "coincidentally" place himself between his teammate and the defender assigned to cover that player. This can happen accidentally, but is more frequently planned.

Piling on. A player deliberately jumping or falling on a ballcarrier or any other player after the whistle has blown the play dead. A fifteen yard penalty results. It can be a judgment call by the official since the perpetrator may have trouble stopping.

Pitch. See **Lateral.**

Place kick. A general term for a kicking method that includes field goal attempts, PATs, and kickoffs. The ball is kicked from a fixed position on the ground. The ball may be held by another player in any situation, but a kicking tee can be used for the kickoff.

Play action pass. A pass play in which a running play is first faked by the offensive team. The purpose is to deceive the defense into bringing the secondary up against the run so the receiver can get free downfield.

Play book. The document that holds all the offensive and defensive plays a team uses. It may also contain notes on individual assignments and information on noted weaknesses of the opposing teams that can be exploited.

Plunge. A maneuver from the backfield in which the fullback takes a handoff from the quarterback and heads for the middle of the offensive line, while the quarterback continues his movement backward and fakes a handoff to the halfback.

Pocket (or **cup**). The protective formation of the offensive linemen around the quarterback as he drops back to pass. The offensive guards try to hold the defensive tackles on the line of scrimmage while the offensive tackles try to force the defensive ends to the outside. The quarterback may have to "step up into the pocket" if the defense begins to close in. This allows the offensive tackles to stay between the defense and the quarterback.

Point-after-touchdown. See **Conversion**.

Pop. A hard hit by either an offensive or defensive player.

Post route. A pass route where the receiver runs downfield and breaks diagonally for the goalpost on his final cut.

Power I. A variation of the I formation. One of the offensive backs lines up in the T formation position behind the offensive tackle, while the other two backs line up behind the quarterback as usual in the I formation. This provides more power on one side of the line.

Power play. Any play in which a blocking back runs to a given hole before the running back with the ball comes through.

Power sweep (or **sweep**). An end run with two linemen leading interference. The sweep develops more slowly than the quick pitch end run.

Prevent defense. A defense designed to prevent a long pass. The defensive backs line up deep to allow the receiver to catch a short pass but not a long one.

Primary receiver. The first-choice receiver a quarterback will try to throw to on a pass play.

Pro-set. See **Open set.**

Pull. An action taken by an offensive lineman in which he steps back quickly and moves in a lateral direction to trap block or lead interference on a sweep.

Pump. A simulated throw by the quarterback used in an attempt to get the defensive backs to move in the wrong direction.

Punt. Kicking the ball over the defending team. Usually on the fourth down when the offense does not believe they can gain sufficient yardage to get a first down and are too far to attempt a field goal. If the punted ball lands untouched, it is dead where it stops and now belongs to the defending team. If it travels into the end zone, it is brought back and spotted on the twenty-yard line. This is called a touchback. If it goes out of bounds it is spotted at that point. If the defending team touches the ball, but does not control it, the ball is free and anybody can claim it. If the punting team is the first team to touch the ball, it is dead and the receiving team takes possession at that point.

Pursuit. The action of the defending team when they are running down the ballcarrier. Good pursuit is necessary for a good defense.

Quarters. There are four quarters to a football game, each consisting of fifteen minutes of playing time. The field end each team defends is switched each quarter.

Quarterback. He calls the plays and is generally the leader of the offense. He is also the primary passer.

Quarterback option (or **quarterback draw**). See **Option pass.**

Quarterback sneak. A play used in short yardage situations in which the quarterback takes the snap from the center and then moves ahead directly forward, behind the center. The offensive line uses wedge blocking on this play.

Quick kick. An offensive team punting unexpectedly by shifting into a short punting formation. It is done in the hope of surprising the defense so they do not have time to get a man downfield to receive the kick. Because surprise is necessary if it is to work, it is usually tried on a third down. A punt would be expected on a fourth down.

Quick opener. Another name for a drive in which the set back goes straight into the line after receiving the handoff from the quarterback.

Quick pass protection. Pass protection in which the offensive linemen go after the defenders directly opposite them on the line in an attempt to get their arms and hands down. It is used when the quarterback is expected to pass quickly after the snap. The line is not expected to provide blocking for as long as they would in a regular pass situation.

Quick release. The term used to describe a quarterback's ability to get rid of the ball quickly after he spots an open receiver.

Reading. See **Keying.**

Red dog. See **Blitz.**

Referee. See **Officials.**

Remaining back. The offensive back who is not carrying the ball on a running play, or not leaving the back field to run a pass route. Usually does some blocking.

Reverse. Any play that starts out going one direction and ends up going in the opposite direction.

Reverse field. A deception play that requires the quarterback to move a short distance with the running back who is faking into the line. The quarterback is said to be "riding" the back into the line.

Rollout. When the quarterback runs quickly to one side or the other before throwing a pass.

Rotation. Movement by the defensive secondary to adjust to the strength of the offensive formation. The rotation may take place before the snap of the ball or after, if they are trying to conceal the defensive formation. Usually associated with a type of zone defense.

Roughing the kicker. The kicker may not be touched after he has kicked the ball. Any contact will result in a penalty unless the ball is touched in the process. It is not an infraction if the defensive player is knocked into the kicker by a member of the kicking team. The penalty is fifteen yards.

Roughing the passer. The passer may not be touched after the ball has left his hands. The referee must use judgment to determine if the defender had a reasonable chance to stop his momentum. The penalty is fifteen yards.

Run pass. See **Option pass.**

Runback. The return of a punt, kickoff, missed field goal, or intercepted pass.

Running back. Any of the offensive backs used primarily to run with the ball.

Rushing. The yardage gained by an offensive team from the line of scrimmage. Yardage gained on kick returns is not included in a team's total rushing yardage statistics.

Rushing the passer. Pursuit by the defense in an attempt to sack the quarterback for a loss of yardage or in an effort to force him to hurry his throw.

Sack. When the quarterback is brought down for a loss of yardage while attempting to pass.

Safety. When a ballcarrier on the offensive team is tackled in his own end zone, or when an attempt to punt out from the end zone is blocked, or if a snap or fumble by the offense rolls out of their end zone. Two points are awarded the defending team for a safety. If a defender intercepts the ball or catches a kick in the end zone, it is a touchback and play is resumed on the twenty yard line. A safety is also the name of the position of one of the deep defensive players.

Safety blitz. When one of the safeties in the defensive backfield leaves his position and charges the offensive line at the snap in an attempt to throw the quarterback for a loss of yardage. See also **Blitz.**

Safety valve. A short pass to one of the set backs when all of the other receivers are covered. This is the safety valve to prevent the quarterback from being thrown for a loss.

Scramble. When the quarterback is forced to leave the pocket and take evasive action after his pass protection has been penetrated by the defense. This differs from a rollout or play pass action in that those are planned actions and the scramble is an improvisation in reaction to the defenders' actions.

Screen pass. The offensive line allows the defense to penetrate and after a short delay forms a wall to screen one of the set backs. The quarterback then throws him a short pass. At the beginning of the play the quarterback drops back as if preparing a long pass. The defense is hopefully conned into believing that their penetration has beaten off the offensive linemen. This play tests the acting abilities of all members of the offensive team.

Scrimmage. The action that takes place from the snap of the ball until the end of the down or until the offensive team loses possession of the ball on any given play. Also: the term used to describe practice under game conditions.

Secondary. The players in the defensive backfield. The secondary consists of the two cornerbacks and the strong and weak safeties. Also: the area beyond the line of scrimmage they are assigned to cover.

Secondary receiver. The receiver the quarterback looks to if the primary receiver cannot get free.

Set back. A general term for the offensive backs that line up behind the quarterback. Usually the fullback and halfbacks, though the term can include the tight end if he lines up behind the quarterback.

Shift. When the offensive backfield moves together from one formation to another before the snap. The shift can involve a single player or many players. Used to keep the opposing team guessing or as a last-minute adjustment to an unexpected formation by the opposing team.

Shoestring tackle. A tackle made around the ballcarrier's ankles.

Shooting the gap. When a defensive lineman tries to run through the space between two offensive linemen without coming into contact with either.

Shotgun formation. A formation in which the quarterback stands alone about seven yards behind the center and takes a direct snap. This is a passing formation and allows the quarterback more time to look for an open receiver. This used to be the way all plays started not too many years ago.

Sidelines. The lines running down the field and marking the sides of the playing field. As with all the lines, the line itself is out of bounds. Also: a pass pattern run toward the outside.

Sideline and go. A pass route in which the receiver runs a sideline route and then breaks deep. The quarterback "pump-fakes" while the sideline route is being run.

Sideline route. The receiver runs down the field and then breaks for the sidelines. Timing is important since the quarterback releases the ball before the break is made.

Slam. When an offensive player makes a shoulder block on a defender and then releases to go downfield and block another player.

Slant play (or **slant-off-tackle,** also **line buck**). An offensive running play in which the back approaches the line of scrimmage at an angle. This gives him an opportunity to break through the line in any of several holes.

Slant route. A pass route in which the receiver runs downfield several yards and then breaks at an angle over the middle.

Slot. The gap in the line between the weak-side tackle and the split end, or between the tight end and the flanker. Receivers are placed in the slot to enable them to get downfield faster and make it more difficult for the defense to double cover one of the wide receivers.

Slot back. Any back lined up in the slot on either side of the line.

Snap. The initiating action of the play by the center when he passes the ball between his legs to the quarterback or placekick holder.

Soccer-style kick. A kicker who approaches the ball diagonally and hits the ball with his instep is a soccer-style kicker. Barefoot kickers are usually soccer-style kickers. Compare to **Straight-on kick.**

Spearing. A deliberate dive by a defensive player headfirst onto an offensive player. A personal foul will be called since this can injure the victim. The heavy football helmet can act as a potent weapon.

Special teams. All of the kicking teams, including the kickoff and kickoff return teams, the punting and punt return teams, and the placekick team. Individual players may be assigned to one or more of the special teams.

Split. The spacing between the offensive linemen. The offense splits to force gaps in the defensive line through which the offensive backs can run.

Split end. Usually a wide receiver, sometimes a blocker, placed on the opposite end of the line from the tight end. The split end and the flanker often perform the same functions and are known collectively as the wide receivers.

Split T formation. A formerly popular offensive formation. It featured large splits in the offensive line and a fast-hitting attack. The defense had trouble adjusting to this formation. When they lined up opposite the offense, huge gaps were created in the defensive line through which the offensive backs could run. The defense also had problems dealing with the fast hitting.

Spotter. A member of the radio or television broadcasting team who identifies the players and feeds the information to the play-by-play announcer. He watches the numbers of the players involved in a play and identifies them by pointing to a chart on which all the players are listed. Also: a member of the scouting team who watches the opposition from the stands.

Spread. The point differential, determined by the professional gambling establishment, which allows the two teams (no matter their individual record or ability) to come into the game at fifty-fifty odds.

Spread formation. See **Shotgun formation.**

Squib. Any kick that doesn't get up in the air, but bounces around on the ground. Not necessarily an onside kick.

Stack. A defensive alignment in which the linebacker lines up directly behind a defensive lineman. The purpose of this alignment is to help them shoot the gaps on each side of the offensive lineman opposite. The linebacker heads to one side and the lineman to the other on the theory that one of them will get through while the offensive lineman is coping with the other.

Stack defense. Any defensive formation in which at least two linebackers are stacked directly behind two defensive linemen.

Straight arm. A maneuver used by a running ballcarrier to fend off an approaching tackler. He extends his arm straight out with the elbow locked and strikes with the heel of his hand at the head of the tackler. Usually used in an open field where there is only one defender to evade and no other alternative.

Straight-on-kick. As the name implies, the kicker approaches the ball from directly upfield and kicks the ball with his toe. Compare to **Soccer-style kick.**

Streak. See **Fly.**

Strong safety. The safety that lines up on the strong side of the line opposing the tight end on the offensive team. In man-to-man coverage, he is usually assigned to cover the tight end.

Strong side. The side of the line where the tight end is positioned. Since there is an extra man on this side, it is called the strong side.

Stunting. See **Games.**

Stunting defense. A type of defense in which the line and the linebackers are involved in stunting much of the time. A stunting defense will usually involve all of the people on the defensive line.

Stutter step. A short, choppy, erratic running action by a running back attempting to avoid a tackler.

Submarine. The action used by a defensive lineman in a short yardage situation when he doesn't want to be forced back off the line of scrimmage. He goes low under or between the offensive lineman opposite him. This maneuver is used when the offense is expected to move straight up the middle. The offense can counter by going up and over the top of the massed tangle of humanity.

Sudden death. The method used to break ties when time has run out. A coin is flipped at the start of the overtime to determine which team will kickoff and which receive. The team that scores first wins. That ends the overtime period.

Suicide squad. A term sometimes used to describe the special teams. The description is a result of the high incidence of injuries on the special teams.

Sweep. See **Power sweep.**

Swing Pass. See **Flare pass.**

T formation. An offensive formation in which the quarterback lines up directly behind the center. The fullback lines up behind the quarterback, and the two halfbacks are set to either side of the fullback forming the top crossbar of the T. The fullback may be slightly deeper on the field than the halfbacks.

Tackle. An offensive lineman positioned between the guard and the end; or a defensive lineman positioned opposite the offensive guards. In either case, the tackles are usually the biggest, baddest men on the field. Also: the maneuver used to bring down a ball carrier.

Tailback. In a single wing formation, the back positioned deepest in the offensive backfield. He is positioned almost directly behind the center.

Tee. See **Kicking tee.**

Three-point stance. The position taken by the players when play is about to begin. The legs are spread and are positioned parallel, the player crouches low and puts one hand on the ground in front of him. This stance allows the player to move out quickly to either side or straight ahead. It is also easy to move from this stance into a block on an opposing player.

Tight end. A player positioned to the outside of the offensive tackle on the line of scrimmage. He is on the same side as the flanker. This is the strong side. The end on the other end of the line is positioned further out from the tackle on that side and is known as the split end. The tight end is used as a blocker or pass receiver.

Timing pattern. A series of routes on a pass play where the various potential receivers make their breaks at different times and different distances down the field. This allows the quarterback to scan the field quickly and determine which receivers are open.

Tip off (or **telegraph**). When certain mannerisms by a player or a team before the play is begun allow the opposition to read the intentions of that team.

Toss of the coin. Before the game begins the referee tosses a coin in the presence of the two team captains. The captain of the visiting team is given the privilege of calling the toss (heads or tails). The winner of the toss has the choice of receiving the opening kickoff or choosing the goal his team will defend for the first quarter. When the second half begins the loser is given the same choice. If the wind is bad the choice of the goal may be more important than receiving the kickoff.

Touchback. Any play in which the ball goes into the end zone untouched on a kick and is either uncaught or not run out. The receiving team takes possession of the ball on the twenty-yard line. If a blocked punt is recovered in the end zone, that is a touchdown. If an offensive player carries the ball into his own end zone on his own momentum he is charged with a safety.

Touchdown. When a player carries the ball into the oppositon's end zone, either by running the ball over the goal line or by catching a pass in the end zone. Worth six points.

Trap. When an offensive lineman pulls back from his position on the line and deliberately allows the defensive lineman to penetrate the line and then blocks the defender to one side.

Trap ball. A call by an official that a pass was incomplete, that the ball touched the ground before the receiver got hold of it. Usually occurs when the pass is short or the receiver is out of position and he makes a diving catch for the ball; he may come up running. This is a difficult call to make as the official must be in exactly the right place to see clearly the moment of contact.

Triple. When three receivers all line up on one side of the line so all three can get downfield.

Turf. Both artificial and real (natural). The ground that a football game is played upon. Traditionally grass—the natural kind that grows in dirt. The latest innovation is artificial turf made of plastic, created originally for the Astrodome since it is difficult to grow the real stuff inside. Astroturf ™ had a boom for a while and then declined in popularity because of injuries. In the future, as enclosed stadiums increase in number, the competition will be between injuries and the need for an indoor turf.

Turn in. A pass route in which the receiver after going downfield turns in toward the middle to catch the ball.

Turn out. A pass route where the receiver after going downfield turns toward the sidelines to catch the ball.

Turnover. When the ball possession changes as a result of a fumble or a pass interception.

Turning the corner. When a player on the offensive team running laterally toward the sidelines turns and starts downfield. Usually applied to the running back carrying the ball.

Two-minute offense. An offensive predetermined series of plays run in the last two minutes of each half. The purpose is to run as many plays as possible when a quick score is needed. Pass plays are usually stressed since they can be run off rapidly and stop the clock when missed. Runs are usually to the sidelines to stop the clock.

Two-minute warning. A time-out called by the field judge when there are two minutes left in the first half and again before the end of the game. In the final two minutes (both halves) the clock does not begin running until the ball has been legally touched by a member of either team. All other times the clock starts when the official thirty second clock starts. A team cannot "buy" an extra time-out even with a delay-of-game infraction. A time-out can be called for an injured player who must be removed from the field immediately. If, as a result of additional injuries, another time-out is needed, it will be called and the team is given a five yard penalty. In addition, if the team that needs the time-out is losing or is tied and has possession, they cannot put the ball into play before ten seconds has run off the clock. The game could end in that ten seconds.

Two-point stance. When a player is "set" (standing or crouching) at the beginning of a play, but does not have a hand on the ground. This stance is used by linebackers, defensive backs, and wide receivers.

Umpire. See **Officials.**

Veer. A running back moving at an angle to either side. His angle and path are usually a result of the defensive flow, but occasionally a play will contain a planned veer for a running back.

Waivers. A player is on waivers if his team has placed him into the system that allows other teams to claim him (or waive the opportunity to do so). This is one part of the procedures set up by the league management to govern trading of players between teams. All the rules are designed to allow the weak teams an advantage in building toward capability.

Weak safety. The safety on the opposite side of the field from the tight end. He may or may not be a free safety.

Weak side. The side of the offensive formation other than the side where the tight end and the flanker are positioned.

Wedge. A kick-off return tactic in which the players of the receiving team form a V-shaped blocking formation in front of the ball carrier.

Wedge breaker. The player on the kickoff team who is assigned the job of separating the wedge of the kickoff return team. He tries to dive into the legs of the players forming the wedge.

Wide receiver. A flanker, split end, or any other receiver set more than six yards from his tight end or offensive tackler.

Wide side. If the ball is spotted on one of the hash marks, the areas between the ball and the sideline farthest from the ball is called the wide side of the field.

Wing. An offensive halfback positioned to the outside of his own end or offensive tackle. If he is "split" out more than a few yards, he is in a slot formation.

Yardage chain. See **Chain.**

Zig in. A pass route in which the receiver runs downfield, cuts to the inside, then cuts to the outside and finally makes a break to the inside again to catch the ball.

Zig out. Same as above except reversed so that the final break is to the outside. Both are designed to confuse the defense as to where the ball will ultimately be thrown.

Zone blocking. When members of the offensive line are assigned to block anyone in a predetermined area of the field. Zone blocking is used as a counter to stunting or games by the defense. Since each player is assigned a specific area or zone, he does not worry about where the man opposing him on the line moves to during the stunt. He blocks any defender that moves into his territory. Zone blocking is easier to use on pass plays, but can be used on running plays also.

Zone defense. A type of coverage by the defensive secondary in which the players are assigned to defend an area or zone of the field rather than being assigned to cover individual receivers.

Index

Dallas Cowboys, 12, 115
Dayton Triangles, 10
Decatur Staleys, 11
defense, 19, 74 – 78, 86
defense holding, 93
delay of game, 91, 97
Dempsey, Tom, 68
Denver Broncos, 12
Detroit Heralds, 11
Detroit Lions, 12, 13
double reverse, 38 – 40
downs, 22
draft choice, 120 – 121
draw, 35
drugs, 122 – 126
encroachment, 91
end around reverse, 37 – 38
end run (sweep), 36 – 37
ends, 19
end zone, 14

face mask, 90
fair catch, 24, 71, 94
field goal, 23, 72 – 94
field judge, 90
first down, 24, 95
first half, 27
flag route, 49 – 52
flare pass, 53 – 54
football field, 13 – 19
formations, 22, 32
forward pass, 43
free agent, 120, 121 – 122
free kick, 26
free recall, 119
fullback, 19

game clock, 26

game plan, 85
goal line, 22 – 23
goal line defense, 77, 78
goalpost, 14
grab and shake tactic, 79
Green Bay Packers, 12, 113
grid lines, 14
Griffith, Andy, 9
groundkeepers, 118
guards, 19

Halas, George, 11, 113
Hammond Pros, 11
Hayes, Woody, 42
head coach, 114 – 115
head linesman, 90
head-up block, 64 – 66
hook pattern, 46
Houston Oilers, 12

incomplete pass, 26
infractions, 91 – 94
injured reserve list, 119
intentional grounding, 28, 93, 106
interference with a fair catch, 94, 100

Kansas City Chiefs, 12
key-reading, 78
kicker, 20
kicking, 68 – 73
kick receiving, 73

line, 19
linebacker, 17
line buck, 34, 35

roughing the kicker, 92, 98
roughing the passer, 84, 92, 104
round robin series, 132
rugby, 67
running into kicker, 92

safeties, 20, 24
San Diego Chargers, 12, 13
San Francisco '49ers, 12
scoring, 21 – 22
scouts, 116
screen pass, 52 – 53
Seattle Hawks, 12
second half, 25, 26
shoulder block, 62
side judge, 90
sideline flag route, 51 – 52
sidelines, 15
signals referee, 94 – 113
slant, 46 – 47
slant off-tackle, 33 – 34
spearing, 66
special teams, 19, 20
St. Louis Cardinals, 12
steroids, 124
strategy, 85 – 87
Super Bowl Game, 134, 135

sweep (end run), 36, 37

tackles, 19
tackling, 79
tactics, 31 – 58
Tampa Bay Buccaneers, 12
three-point stance, 60, 61
tie-breaking rules, 133
time-out, 26 – 27, 96
touchback, 24
touchdown, 21 – 22, 11
trap, 36
triple option, 40 – 41
turf, 17 – 18
two-minute drill, 28

umpire, 89
unsportsmanlike conduct, 94

waiver recall, 119
waiver system, 120
Washington Redskins, 12
wild-card team, 132 – 133
wishbone-T formation, 40

yardage, 74

zebras (officials), 88 – 91
zone defense, 81 – 82